Louis Compton Miall

Thirty Years of Teaching

Louis Compton Miall

Thirty Years of Teaching

ISBN/EAN: 9783337165475

Printed in Europe, USA, Canada, Australia, Japan

Cover: Foto ©Paul-Georg Meister /pixelio.de

More available books at **www.hansebooks.com**

THIRTY YEARS OF TEACHING.

BY

L. C. MIALL, F.R.S.,

PROFESSOR OF BIOLOGY IN THE YORKSHIRE COLLEGE.

*REPRINTED, WITH ADDITIONS,
FROM THE JOURNAL OF EDUCATION*

London:
MACMILLAN AND CO., Limited,
NEW YORK: THE MACMILLAN COMPANY.
1897.

All rights reserved.

GLASGOW: PRINTED AT THE UNIVERSITY PRESS
BY ROBERT MACLEHOSE AND CO.

CONTENTS.

	PAGE
PERSONAL EXPLANATIONS,	1
THE NECESSITY OF BEING INTERESTING,	2
MAXIMS FOR LECTURERS,	6
PLENTY OF CONCRETE ILLUSTRATIONS,	9
CONCRETE ILLUSTRATIONS OF ENGLISH HISTORY,	10
REWARDS AND PUNISHMENTS,	16
HELPLESSNESS AND HANDINESS,	22
FINDING OUT AND BEING TOLD,	33
PLAIN SPEECH,	41
SCHOOL HOURS,	46
HOW TO MAKE ROOM FOR ALL THE SUBJECTS WHICH ARE TO BE TAUGHT IN SCHOOLS,	53
THE TEACHING OF SUBJECTS AND THE TEACHING OF SCHOLARS,	66
LECTURING AND TEACHING,	82
READING ALOUD IN THE FAMILY,	90
SCHOOL LESSONS IN DRAWING,	92

	PAGE
GEOGRAPHY AND MAP-DRAWING,	96
ARITHMETICAL PRECISION,	98
ELEMENTARY GEOMETRY,	110
CLASSICAL GRAMMAR ON LITERATURE,	123
SCHOOL MUSEUMS,	138
EXAMINERS AND CANDIDATES,	145
A DIALOGUE ON PEDAGOGY AND PSYCHOLOGY,	152
THE TRAINING OF A GREAT NATURALIST,	171
THE EDGEWORTHS ON PRACTICAL EDUCATION,	197
NATURE-STUDY,	209
REMARKS ON TWO PASSAGES IN BAIN'S "EDUCATION AS A SCIENCE,"	225
FROEBEL AND PESTALOZZI,	234
INDEX,	248

THIRTY YEARS OF TEACHING.

PERSONAL EXPLANATIONS.

ANY man who has practised a profession for thirty years ought to have gained experience useful to his juniors. Whether he can communicate his experience or not depends upon certain personal qualities of which he himself is the worst possible judge. Though I have taught in schools and have always kept up a more or less close connexion with schools, my ordinary occupation has been that of a lecturer. This is against my present attempt. Lecturing is easier than teaching, and it does not concern nearly so many people. Moreover, the habit of lecturing inevitably produces an unpleasant dogmatic manner. I must try to be on my guard against this.

THE NECESSITY OF BEING INTERESTING.

If we would make our pupils or students into allies and not into enemies, we must interest them in the subject. This can always be done if three conditions are satisfied. First, the subject must be worth teaching; secondly, the pupil must be fit to learn; thirdly, the teacher must be fit to teach. As to the subject, I should say that every subject is interesting which is not artificially restricted. You can make geography dry by restricting it to boundaries and population and names of chief towns. You can make history dry by restricting it to dates and the chief events of each reign. But it is nevertheless true, as Macaulay said, that every subject has its interesting side if you can only find it out.

Here I can fancy some teacher breaking in with the remark: "But I don't want to be always interesting. I don't wish my pupils to need external excitement. They ought to be drilled. They ought to be trained to face drudgery, to go through tiresome calculations, to get up dry details and obscure events." Yes, that is true also, but not in any sense which contradicts the necessity of being interesting, to which I unflinchingly adhere. It is my business, for example, to study details which, to most people, would seem stupid and dry in the highest degree. I occupy myself with the variations in shape of the mandibles and maxillæ and antennæ of insects. I delight in working out new details of legs and wings. What led me to this? Why do I care about variations in form which to another seem totally unimportant? Because I am interested in the subject. Years ago I was led to see that attention to these details would help to solve questions in which Darwin and Huxley, and other men who had the true gifts of the teacher, had given me an enduring interest. It is no drudgery to me to work out minute details so long as the inspiration of my masters continues in full force. Were that to fail, were I once reduced to enumeration of parts, without any sense of the results to be attained, I should give up natural history forthwith. Hard work without interest, without inspiration, without hope of gratifying one's curiosity, would have no more attraction for me than work without wages would have for a collier. Interest me sufficiently, and I will struggle with any details, however laborious; but without interest in my work I am paralysed. Nor have I ever met a man decently successful in any pursuit which could be called intellectual who was not interested in it. Dogged work from a sense of duty, without eagerness or enthusiasm, will suffice for some things, but not for these. We make progress in history, in mathematics, in languages, very nearly in proportion to the interest which we take in them, so that I think I am right in saying that we absolutely must interest our pupils if we are to do any good with them.

De Morgan tells us that in order to establish the superiority of Horner's method of solving cubic equations he proposed to his class to work out results extending to more than fifty places of decimals as a Christmas exercise. He got answers of 75, 65, 63, 58, 57 and 52 places. One went to 101 places. Subsequently another pupil carried the result to 152 places. That is the kind of interest we want to rouse. Depend upon it, the teaching which led these young men to undertake such toilsome computations had some fire in it.

How can we make our subject interesting?— is a question to which there are scores of answers, none adequate. A sound method, a lively style, terse language, are all good things. Yet one writer shall fail in spite of possessing them all, while another shall succeed without one of them. Turn over Goldsmith's "Essays," and see if you can tell why they succeeded, while the other hacks of Griffiths and Newbery, using the same artifices, failed. The public felt the difference in a moment, and so do we more than a century later, but few of us would undertake to say in what the trick consists.

Still the explanation is not altogether hidden from us. Criticism has brought to light some few principles, which may be a guide, though not an infallible test. I think that we may name one or two qualities which are apt to bring luck. I should put first of all what a painter calls *breadth*. Whatever subject you handle, go for simplicity of impression. If you bring in many details, make them help one another. It is deadly in the lesson or the lecture to insist upon details merely because they are in the books, or because they are valued by the expert. We must continually ask: "Why do I teach this? Is it really important that my pupils should know about it?" A sound judgment as to what is and what is not important cannot be got by taking pains. Those who have it by nature will be saved from one of the worst mistakes which a teacher commonly makes—I mean *pedantry*, putting trivial distinctions in the first place and practical command of the subject in the second.

We cannot expect every teacher to possess either the leisure or the faculty necessary to advance the subjects which he professes. If, by chance, he should be an original authority, he enjoys a rare advantage—provided, however, that he has worked at his subject like a man, not burying himself in obscure details. To bore us with small matters that don't signify is a privilege that we unwillingly grant to any man, however eminent. But it now and then happens to nearly all of us to listen to a real discoverer, who has by hard labour achieved results of permanent value—such, I mean, as gratify an enlightened curiosity, or tend to the relief of man's estate. How memorable may be the words and gestures of such a man, if only he escapes being absolutely inarticulate! A very little of this power of working for himself gives to the teacher of whatever grade a weight that no facility of language can match.

Don't, if you are a teacher, covet facility and grace of speech too eagerly. Above all, distrust such faculty of abundant extempore speech as you may chance to possess. Fluency, an impressive manner, a happy choice of words, and so on, joined to that hatred of hard work which afflicts almost all men, go far towards making an impostor. Never mind that you are slow of speech, or that it costs you much study to put your notions into a moderately effective shape. The teacher does not need brilliancy; he is all the better without facility. Of the gifts of the orator none are required except that he should speak up and sound his consonants.

MAXIMS FOR LECTURERS.

What immediately follows relates to lecturing, and not to class-teaching. I intend now and then to claim the lax methods of the reminiscent.

It has been my lot to be bored extensively by lectures, and to bore other people in return. All the time, but especially when listening to other people's lectures, I have tried to find out and define the causes of boredom. Thirty years of combined suffering and infliction justify me in laying down a few simple rules, which I bequeath to posterity.

1. Make no introductory remarks. Let your first sentence belong to the exposition of your subject. Never say why you consented to lecture, nor why you chose that particular subject. Remarks on the shortness of the time are great wasters of time. I have heard of a clergyman who had to address a Church Congress under a strict ten minutes' rule. His ten minutes were spent in deploring the shortness of the time. Then a bell rang, and the astonished performer had to sit down with even his excuses unfinished. Probably he thought that he had been robbed of about nine minutes. Let your last sentence, like your first, belong to the exposition of your subject. Perorations are as tiresome as introductions. I have often found that the closing paragraphs of a lecture or paper, in which the author ventures to draw a moral or trace a natural law, are either irrelevant or untrue.

2. (This is hard.) Fix a time-limit beforehand, or, better still, get some one else to fix it for you, and sit down when it is reached, whether you have done or not. A lecturer at the Royal Institution, who had been pointedly warned not to exceed his hour, sat down abruptly when the clock struck, though he was by no means through with his discourse. He was congratulated on hitting the time so exactly, but, to his mortification, no one remarked that his concluding sentences had been shorn off. People will forgive you anything if you will only leave off promptly. It is miserable to see a man agonising for five minutes.

3. Settle the plan of your lecture exactly in your mind, and also the wording of the important sentences. Leave the rest to take such shape as it can.

4. Don't tell all that you know about your subject. Don't even touch upon all the topics which suggest themselves. *Le secret d'ennuyer est celui de tout dire* (Voltaire).

5. Unless you are a master of speech, never attempt to bring in fine passages. The spoken style is, or ought to be, simple in construction; and carefully prepared passages, written out and committed to memory, will not weave in with the rest.

PLENTY OF CONCRETE ILLUSTRATIONS.

Children, young people, and most men and women, are more easily interested in what is actual and concrete than in what is theoretical and abstract. There are, of course, exceptions. I once heard a man complain of being distracted by certain optical experiments. The readiest way into his mind was through equations. But most people love particulars and circumstance. How does this agree with what was said just now about the necessity of *breadth*? It agrees perfectly well, provided that the particulars illustrate one another—that they converge to produce an impression of growing simplicity and force. Isolated details may be tiresome to any extent; it is the building-up of the details into a picture or an argument that is interesting, and the highest pitch of interest is reached when a number of facts, apparently unconnected, are made to fit neatly into their places. It is like fitting together mosaic, or restoring a shattered vase. But let us not be mastered by our own cleverness, as happens to some brilliant people. Human nature likes now and then to coax the facts just a little. The theory would be so complete if this inconvenient fact were dropped; the pieces of the vase would go together so much better if this unnecessary corner were broken off. By all that is honourable, resist that temptation! If you yield, it will make a charlatan of you. Those ugly facts will become necessary before the problem is truly solved. That corner which you would like to break off has a space to fill, which must be filled before the vase can be truly restored. No man, perhaps, ever respected inconvenient facts so heartily as our great naturalist, Charles Darwin. I believe that his singular power in the interpretation of nature depended largely upon his determination to give the angular fragments fair play. Awkward facts, which he would neither drop nor coerce, led him to some of his best results.

History is most intelligible to average people when it is most biographical. Geography becomes most intelligible when it includes a profusion of the details which can be drawn or photographed. Mathematics becomes most intelligible when it is employed to work out mechanical or astronomical results. Interest and intelligibility are not everything, but for young and untrained minds they are the chief thing.

CONCRETE ILLUSTRATIONS OF ENGLISH HISTORY.

Let me try to illustrate the value of actual and concrete facts in the teaching of English History. Among the many books which call themselves

"School Histories of England" are some meagre epitomes without one interesting remark or one lively story. All the details upon which a child's imagination can fix are left out. This is the result of a purely mechanical method. So many pages, and no more, can be allotted to a thousand years. Later centuries are allowed a larger space than more ancient ones. A rule-of-three sum gives say ten or twenty pages to a particular reign. Into that space you must contrive to get every event that can be fairly included in a school examination paper. There is the king's title to trace, the battles to mention, with their dates and their results. The substance of the chief Acts of Parliament must be given, and there must be notices of the life of the people, the literature, the science, and the fine art of the time. Working up your material with pains and impartiality on this rule-of-three method, you get a kind of historical glue.

How then should the history of England be taught to young people? To begin with, we must claim more time in class and more time for preparation by the teacher than many schools will concede. If the time in class is limited to two hours a week, and if the teacher has to give five lessons a day on various subjects, there is perhaps nothing better than to stick to the historical glue. But if you can get English history taught in school by men and women who know their subject decently, and if they are not compelled to pace their rounds like horses in a mill, there is a better way open to them.

We want to bring the minds of the scholars into the closest possible contact with the facts. That means study of the narratives of eye-witnesses, and illustration by photographic copies of maps, portraits, scenery, ancient writings, and ancient coins. Suppose that the subject is the reign of George II. Its adequate illustration involves passages from Horace Walpole, plates by Hogarth, a copy of Dance's portrait of Clive, maps of ever so many countries, plans of ever so many battles. Photographic lantern-slides will help you, so will all the knowledge of men and books and arts and countries that you have been able to pick up. But the preparation will be laborious, and the class will not get on fast. Real teaching has to be paid for, in time, and money, and labour.

So elaborate a provision is not necessary in the case of junior forms. But here too the details preserved in the narratives of eye-witnesses must come in, if the story is to impress the children in the right way. There is no sound way of sparing labour, or getting it done for you once for all. We want to develop the historic imagination of our pupils, and that can only be done by helping them bit by bit to build up a true mental picture of each great historic period. The verbal memory can be trusted for such facts as *Charles II., 1660*, but it is only the historic imagination, acting upon a vast collection of facts, which can present such a picture, so vivid and so useful, as Macaulay's "State of England under Charles II." What Macaulay, with his unrivalled knowledge and brilliant power of description, did for that age we must try to do in a far humbler way for other ages. The greatest help of all is wide reading among the narratives of eye-witnesses. It will save a little trouble to some people if I give a short list of such narratives as are easily accessible to every teacher.

> Fitzstephen's Description of London. Translated in Stowe's Survey.
> Chronicle of Jocelyn of Brakelond. In Latin. Published by the Camden Society. An English translation has appeared under the title of Monastic and Social Life in the Twelfth Century, by T. E. Tomlins (London, 1844). See also Carlyle's Past and Present.
> The Paston Letters.
> Narrative of Antony Delaber. In Foxe's Book of Martyrs, and Froude's History of England.
> Roper's Life of Sir Thomas More.
> Cavendish's Life of Wolsey.
> Sir Philip Warwick's Memoirs of King Charles.
> Siege of Lathom House (Bohn's Library).

Memoirs of Colonel Hutchinson (Bohn's Library).
Autobiography of Joseph Lister (Civil War time).
Pepys' Diary (Bohn's Library).
Evelyn's Diary (Bohn's Library).
Thoresby's Diary.
Calamy's Life and Times.
Horace Walpole's Letters. The whole correspondence is very bulky. Some interesting extracts are given in Seeley's Life and Times of Horace Walpole.
Boswell's Life of Johnson.

Few parts of England are distant from all places of historic interest, and many places (London, Oxford, York, Exeter, Salisbury, Newcastle, Norwich, Shrewsbury, etc.) abound in interesting relics of the past, or have them within reach of a short journey. It should be a first object with the enterprising teacher of English history to visit with his class all that is interesting and accessible in this way; to study the topography, the architecture, the heraldic bearings, and to bring away rubbings or photographs.

The order of the chief events, their connexion with contemporary foreign history, and especially what we may call the sense of historical *scale*, are pleasantly got by preparing in class a historical chart.

Suppose that the history of England, from the Norman Conquest to the accession of James I., is to occupy a school form for one year. I should hang up in the class-room a chart, say six feet long. This chart is to be divided into vertical columns, each devoted to a particular country, English or foreign, or, if less detail is necessary, into two columns only, one for England, and one for the rest of the world. The six feet of length have to cover 537 years, about a foot to a century. Divide each foot into ten equal spaces. The more important events can be written in as they come up. Coloured ink pencils are suitable for writing on a vertical surface, and the different colours can be turned to account to represent constitutional, ecclesiastical, military, and other classes of events. Such a chart gives a truer and more vivid impression of the duration of periods than mere numbers can do, and, as I know by actual experience, prevents those absurd mistakes of whole centuries, which harrow up the soul of the faithful teacher. The chart is excellent for recapitulation in class.

I have seen such charts printed ready for use in class, and crowded with obscure details. My advice would be to let the chart grow under the eyes of the class, and to exclude all that the class is not interested in. It should be rather a brief reminder of work done than an ambitious programme.

REWARDS AND PUNISHMENTS.

Let us have as few of either kind as possible. Interest in the work is the substitute to which we should look. In our age, public opinion is continually interposing to mitigate the violence and frequency of punishment. I wish all success to public opinion. It seems to me wrong that the teacher should carry a cane, wrong that he should inflict punishment in haste, wrong that punishment should light upon the stupid child merely because he is stupid. In our colleges the older boys and girls, only just emancipated from the cane or the imposition, need no punishment at all. It is true that they are older and wiser; it is also true that the worst material of the school never enters college at all. Still the total change in method is noteworthy. The mild discipline of the college might surely be relied upon a little more in the school.

What is to be done with idle and uninterested scholars? In extreme cases, and after fair trial, they should certainly be excluded. But this is a remedy to be applied sparingly. One or two per cent. of exclusions in the year will act powerfully enough, where the character of the school stands so high that it is felt to be a privilege to attend it. Then there are the interminable cases of untidiness, thoughtlessness, and neglect—not gross, not

REWARDS AND PUNISHMENTS. 17

systematic. Good-natured boys, popular with their fellows, shirk their lessons or eat apples in school. Are you to keep them in, or to cane them, or to let them go on in impunity? I should like to give a piece of actual experience bearing on this point.

In a school where detentions had grown to a discouraging extent, it was at length decided to set up a tell-tale to signify at a glance what boys were in trouble. A large frame was set up in the schoolroom, and on this every boy had his own tablet, a piece of wood about ten inches by two inches, with the boy's name on both sides, black on one side and white on the other. The tablets could be reversed by rotation on pivots. When a boy had a lesson rejected, or an imposition set, his tablet was turned, and remained so till the work was cleared off. It was easy to see at a glance who was liable to detention, and this increased the certainty of the penalty. Moreover, some one had to stay in charge till all was cleared off, and the tell-tale acted as an efficient check upon thoughtless and exorbitant punishments. Before long both masters and boys began to feel the irksomeness of an unusually black list, and the satisfaction to be derived from a maiden assize. Any master who was profuse with his punishments had to encounter a hostile public opinion, and was felt to manage worse than those who kept order

B

without unusual severity. Before long, a further extension was tried. It was determined that any boy who got no mark of disgrace for a whole term should have his tablet screwed down, and his name written up in gold letters. So long as it remained thus, he was exempt from all penalties whatsoever. That privilege was abused in no single instance. The unexceptionable class was very small, and a gentle hint sufficed for them.[1]

Most of us know by bitter experience how the schoolboy's life may be poisoned by unjust punishment. I once got one hundred lines of Virgil for a trifling offence of which I was not guilty. The master who gave the lines was convinced, ten minutes later, that he had taken one boy for another, but (foolish man that he was!) he could not bring himself to acknowledge his mistake, and merely omitted to call for the last half of the lines. That piece of injustice made me a rebel for months. Punishment should never be hasty—one reason, and there are many more, against the cane or the box on the ear. It should be deliberate and restrained, like the decisions of a judge.

A word upon indiscriminate punishment—that is, the punishment of the guilty and innocent

---

[1] This plan was successfully carried out in the school formerly conducted by Mr. George Todd, at Stamford Hill.

alike. Sometimes a window is broken, or a caricature of the master chalked up on the blackboard. The offender is not to be found. The class is threatened with punishment if he is not given up. Still no result. Then the threat is carried into effect, and the whole class is kept in on Saturday afternoon. Is this just?

I am inclined to think that such indiscriminate punishments violate the elementary principles of justice. The case quoted looks, at first sight, like the not unfamiliar case in which a community, governing itself under municipal laws, accepts a certain responsibility for the acts of its members, even when such acts cannot be brought home to individuals. But the boys of a school-class are not self-governing. They have no police functions, and do not wish to undertake them. It is surely unjust to treat them as having a will of their own in one particular emergency only, viz., when the schoolmaster is unable to discover an offender. Nor is it fair that the schoolmaster should, by an exercise of mere authority, give them a motive for discovering the offender. If the class is not responsible to begin with, it cannot be made responsible by a threat.

Anyone who exercises authority should bear in mind: (1) that he is not justified in punishing the innocent; (2) that he is not justified in punishing the guilty before conviction. These principles are of greater importance than the convenience of the schoolmaster, and must not be violated merely to get him out of a difficulty. I have known cases in which boys have suffered indiscriminate punishment who had no direct knowledge of the offence or of the offender. The injustice here becomes palpable, though not, I think, greater than before.

It is possible to imagine cases in which the schoolboy, or anyone of like status, may be morally bound to throw aside *esprit de corps*, and to give in the name of an offender. The schoolboy is not merely a schoolboy; he is also a member of society. But cases sufficiently serious to justify such an appeal are happily rare. They would, in general, justify criminal proceedings against the offender, if known, or at least his immediate removal from the school. The schoolboy will not readily be impressed with the gravity of such cases. He goes by simple rules, and does not draw distinctions. *Not to tell tales* is one article of the school code, and the schoolmaster will not easily gain obedience to commands which infringe it. He must be just and patient if he is, even on a special occasion, to prevail over a tradition of such authority, which, in ordinary circumstances, is so well adapted to the school commonwealth.

The teacher will do well never to make ill-natured or sarcastic remarks. Occupying a position which exempts him from reply or open criticism, he should, above all things, be fair to those under him. Sarcasm becomes base and cowardly when the power of retort is taken away. Grave rebuke, or good-humoured exposure of an absurdity, does no harm; but the teacher must not use biting words. If he pours contempt upon those who cannot defend themselves, he may look for deterioration in himself, and the hatred of his temporary subjects.

Our rewards are sometimes extravagantly high. I cannot see the sense of giving a boy or young man a substantial income for two or three years merely because he has passed a certain examination with credit. The public creates scholarships and fellowships in order to help poor and deserving students. Very often it is the rich and deserving student who carries them off. I should like to see the benevolent intention realized, though without profusion. One way would be to offer bursaries to needy students who on private inquiry were found to show fair promise. A still better way of befriending the poor student would be to make grants towards a general reduction of the fees in particular places of secondary education. All the scholarships and fellowships in the British Isles are less important as a stimulus to higher studies than the reduction (could we only manage it) of the fees of tuition in our University colleges to a maximum charge of £10 a year. Cheap education for every one, and not prizes to the few, is what is wanted to give every promising youth a fair chance.

HELPLESSNESS AND HANDINESS.

A little while ago the girls in a certain high school were busy with a Christmas dramatic entertainment. The dresses were naturally a chief point of interest. A lady friend and one of the teachers undertook between them to superintend the choice of materials and the cutting-out. When the work was half finished the teacher fell ill, and the friend was called away. The dresses were stopped, in spite of such help as a hundred girls and ten grown-up women could render. One girl alone ventured to try some rather desperate expedients, which turned out ill, and caused loss of time. But for the speedy recovery of the skilled teacher, the dresses could not have been finished in time. My informant, who was an eye-witness, tells me that a notable feature of the school in question is that the time of the boarders is absolutely filled up, with the exception of an hour or two on Sunday afternoons, and that this is done to prevent the girls from getting into mischief. Work, play, out-of-door games, gymnastics, walks

—all are arranged by the staff. Teachers are told off for every emergency. There are no sprained ankles, or dirty pinafores, *and there is not a girl in the whole school who can cut out a dress.*

Helplessness is not peculiar to girls, nor to particular schools. In any miscellaneous collection of boys or girls you will find some handy and others helpless. Some are venturous and full of resource; others ready to despair of an unusual experiment, unable to work to a description or drawing, unwilling to tackle a problem of any sort whatever. Send out children to search for carefully described flowers in places where they are known to grow: some will almost always succeed; others will almost always fail.

"When we cannot get paint-brushes for our maps," said a child to me, "there are three things which we can make do. The best is the brush from father's gum-pot; the next best is some of sister's hair, tied about a match; the worst is a piece of paper wound round into a spill." I call a child handy that will work with such tools rather than be hindered altogether. There are both helpless and handy men and women, and that in almost all callings. Grown men, used to tools from boyhood, may be afraid to step out of their routine. A cabinet-maker said to me of one of his men: "He is neither clever, nor careful, nor steady, but I have kept him for many years, because he is the only man in the place who can think. All the others go to him when they get fast." But experience of the right sort counts for something, too. An old salt is pretty sure to be handy and full of resource. A man-of-war's man who served under me for some fifteen years would tackle the most unexpected difficulties. I tried him at joinery, white-washing, house-painting and papering, hatching eggs in an incubator, making glazed cases, and a score of other things, and never knew him to refuse a job merely because he had not tried such a thing before. "In the Navy we are taught to turn our hands to anything that is wanted," was his explanation. The helpless are fond of undertaking to "do their best." I have been sometimes provoked into saying: "Do it—don't do your best!"

How are helpless and handy people made, and where do they come from? I have not attended to the matter long enough to quote a sufficient number of well-investigated cases. The few families which I can speak about from personal knowledge do not, however, yield a single case of feeble and utterly non-inventive people coming of enterprising and skilful parents. It is pretty certain that these qualities follow the common rule as stated by Francis Galton. Parentage, we may fairly suppose, counts for a great deal;

training counts for a great deal too. Whether the influence of the parents is directly transmitted, or works by example only, is a question which need not occupy us here. I conclude that where ingenuity and handiness are daily exercised the children of the household can hardly fail to get them in some degree, and that helplessness is a reproach either to the parents, or to the school, or to both.

The new boy at school! I look back forty years, and see him standing in the midst of a crowd of noisy urchins, turned into the lavatory to wash for dinner. He was dressed, I rather think, in black, and I have a suspicion that his father was a clergyman, lately dead. I remember his pale face, his neat dress and hair, and his white hands. He and all the surrounding objects come before me as bathed in sunshine. How is it that the pictures of boyhood are painted (in my case, at least) in colours, and that the sun seems to have been always shining then? The scenes of the last ten years are monochromatic, and the sky is always clouded. I see the impatient boys whipping off their jackets, plying soap and water, huddling up the hasty wash with a hasty wipe, and taking out the rest of the time in fooling. The new boy, when he finds an unoccupied basin, goes timidly up to it, without taking off his coat, dips his fingers in, and wets his face. Then he stands still as if waiting for the maid to bring a towel. But there is no maid, and when he realizes that his wet face and hands will not be dried for him he bursts into tears. The poor mother who saw day after day that he was washed and brushed, and fondly hoped that she was giving him habits of tidiness—how little she realized that her boy of eight or nine would endure the misery of the helpless! The rest of the history I have forgotten. Whether the boy was more or less tidy than his fellows in the end I do not know, but he had to pick up the knowledge of how to wash and dress himself in a rough-and-tumble fashion, with no help or direction whatever.

Here is a chapter of more recent history. Two boys of eight and seven, very well known to me, had been taught to do as much as possible for themselves, to wash and dress, to clear away for themselves after meals, and to help a little in the house. A domestic interregnum was on hand, and there was no servant in the house. The mother knew that she must get up early and make breakfast ready. When she got to the foot of the stairs at seven o'clock in the morning, she saw the little boys dancing up and down before her in the hall, and became aware that something unusual was afoot. Going down to the kitchen, she found a bright fire, a clean hearth, and a kettle of boiling water. In the breakfast-room the cloth was laid and the places set. The boys had done all that was wanted, and enjoyed the triumph of having saved their mother all that trouble.

Our school and home training does little to encourage handiness. Book-work and paper-work fill the day. Home-lessons fill the evening—book-work and paper-work again. Some unfortunate children have their time filled up of set purpose, lest forsooth they should get into mischief! If they were children of mine, I had rather they broke windows and tore knickerbockers than that they should be kept out of mischief by having their whole time occupied. The very play of the children has everything taken out of it which can stimulate their ingenuity. Take the boy's bat, wickets, cricket-ball, football, or the girl's doll and doll's house as examples. *They are all bought ready-made.* No room for contrivance, or for the adaptation of natural materials, no room for dexterity with the pocket-knife, which was still relied upon a good deal by the schoolboys of my generation. Forty years ago we used to make our sailing-boats out of the squared log, rig them for ourselves, cut out the leaden keel, and nail it on for ourselves. We used to make whistles out of the rowan-tree, and sledges, all but the iron wheels. So far as I can see, the schoolboy of to-day buys all such things ready for use. But the change is not all for the worse. Some schools have their workshops, and teach the boys to be workmanlike. I could wish that they would now and then set little practical problems as well. The work should not all be done to pattern.

Do you want to know whether your own boys and girls are being brought up to be handy or helpless? You have only to notice whether you can keep your gum-pot in your study, the hammer and nails in the kitchen drawer. Handy children will not be debarred from implements so invaluable. Gum, nails, screws, wire, string seem more precious to a handy child than learning, or fresh air, or bread. What if you have no gum-pot, no hammer, no wire? I am afraid that in such case neither you nor your children are handy.

How are we to encourage handiness? It should by rights be taught to the children from the time of their first recollections. Handiness should be taught in the nursery. A little later we have the schoolmaster to contend with. If only he would drop the home-lessons! If he won't do that, and he hardly will in our time, you must come to terms with him, and manage to rescue a good bit of leisure time for the young ones. Then it is for you to find them materials and notions and encouragement. I will give you the experience of one nursery and schoolroom, in which a girl and three boys educated themselves in handiness. I will engage to mention nothing, without express warning, that has not been successfully tried. Map-making, gardening, fret-work, wood-carving, joinery, are first-rate occupations, which I pass over with mere mention because they are well known, and regularly taught in some few households and schools.

Printed Letters.—Get from the stationer gummed sheets printed with alphabets of letters. Various sizes of large type are desirable, but one will be enough at first. A hundred copies will not be too many. Give these out, one or a few at a time, for cutting up. Squares of paste-board, ready cut, are a valuable accessory, and will make movable letters for games of spelling. The ingenuity of the children will ultimately devise all kinds of applications—titles of large maps, mimic posters, names of beasts in the menagerie, etc.

The Menagerie.—The animals should be painted, cut out, and set up in paper cages with thread wires. Encourage the children to trace the outline before they are able to draw. Tracing-paper should always be at command where children are busy. Never mind about the scale of the creatures. The elephant and the porcupine satisfy the child's mind if both are of the same size. I remember what delight my young ones got out of the paper menagerie, with its decorations and night-light illuminations, how eager they were to see the real creatures in the travelling show, and how carefully they noted points for home use.

Paper Books for School Use.—"Having exiled the slate, which gives opportunity for many small bad habits, the school secures a very valuable occupation by making paper books for its various forms of writing and counting exercise. To fold and cut the paper from sheets ruled with lines at various distances, to count, cover, and sew these leaves into books, gives a wide variety of very simple practice for accuracy of eye and neatness of hand. As a moral by-help to careful usage and respect for public property, the reflection, We made the books ourselves, and we know their value, comes of itself, as we say."[1] I have not tried this, but should certainly do so if I kept school.

Paper Work.—Every child ought to learn how to make a variety of paper boxes, for keeping caterpillars in, and so on.

Scrap Book.—A large, strongly-bound scrap book should be at hand to receive cut-out pictures, printed scraps from the newspaper, etc.

Mounting Dried Plants.—This teaches quite a variety of minor industries, and is invaluable for practice in minute accuracy of several kinds.

[1] W. H. Herford, "The School," p. 9.

Decorations.—Christmas should be observed in the nursery by fixing up transparencies, illuminated mottoes, etc. We have discouraged things done for us by the lithographer, and have helped the children to find out ways for themselves. Father Christmas can be dressed up with great effect. A big hollow ship, made in the house, and laden with sweetmeats, raisins, and little gifts, is a pleasant alternative with the Christmas-tree.

Doll's House.—Buy your little girl a wooden cupboard with folding doors and a shelf. Let her paper it inside, and make or adapt all the furniture. What wonderful black-leaded grates I have seen—all cut out of paper.

When the children are thirteen or fourteen, these simple, childish occupations lose their charm. We now propose such things as follow:—

Cabinet of Minerals and Fossils.—Neat naming and scrupulous tidiness are required. This leads very naturally to the next occupation.

Cardboard Models of Crystals.—I should hardly have ventured to put this down if one of my boys had not taken so much pleasure in it. Exactness in measuring and cutting are indispensable.

Photography.—Where this is an established occupation of an older member of the family, it makes plenty of delightful work for the young ones. Printing, trimming, and sorting the paper-prints are just in their way. Let the elder children design Christmas cards and adorn them with pictures, borders of natural foliage, etc. The family photographer will then be called in to help, and the children, once supplied with the negatives, can do all the rest.

Costumes.—A little dramatic scene will give amusement to boys and girls for weeks. The girls will learn to make fancy dresses, the boys to shape dragons, masks, etc., out of pasteboard and tinsel. It is just as easy, where French or German is being sensibly taught, to learn a good piece of the foreign language at the same time.

Pendulum Curves.—A boy of mechanical turn can set up the whole thing for himself, and will be much the better for it.

Easy Scientific Experiments.—I can only find time for one, which I mention because it may well come very early. Fill a bottle with water, cork it tightly, and wire it. Put it in the garden (not near a window) during a hard frost, and then listen for the report of the bursting. Many variations may be tried. Take an open glass cylinder, say six inches high and an inch and a half wide. Fill it to within an inch of the top with water, and dust the surface of the water with powdered charcoal. After freezing a good many hours the layer of charcoal will be found to be frozen into the ice not at the surface, but some distance below. Why is this?

The merits of tidiness are not always appreciated in schools. I have seen more than one bright and enthusiastic science-master, whose apparatus lay anyhow in the class-room. You could not handle anything without soiling your fingers. What trouble there is in store for the pupils so trained! The most deplorable untidiness sometimes proceeds from false economy; the teachers are too busy to keep things in good order, and no helps are provided. An untidy class-room or laboratory can never be thoroughly efficient.

FINDING OUT AND BEING TOLD.

Teachers who understand their business often quote some such rule as this:—"Never tell the child what he can find out for himself." There is no rule more difficult to keep. The bad teacher breaks it always; his lessons are framed on a contrary rule. The good teacher breaks it now and then, from lack of time, or from thoughtlessness, or even of set purpose. After all the rule is but a rule, and the teacher is a free man. He will not bind himself by rules. Nevertheless, the better the teacher the more scrupulously will he keep this one. Experience and patient study of methods will make it possible for him to observe the rule where a less attentive teacher would infallibly break it.

Taken as a literal rule, hard and unflinching, it is impossible and unnatural. All rules are so, where the minds of a number of human beings are concerned. The best of teachers will tell a class some fact in natural history, when he might have taken them into the fields to observe it for themselves. The fact is wanted there and then; to observe it directly would cost half a day; to omit all mention of it would be to omit a necessary qualification of an important principle which is being worked out. If we are to make our natural science absolutely for ourselves, we must be prepared to spend some centuries upon it.

The literal rule is not only impracticable: it is also unnatural. Weary of piling up dead facts and applying dead formulæ, the impatient thinker is, I admit, at times inclined to revolt. "Let us have no facts or formulæ brought in from without: let us work, no matter how slowly, for ourselves." A too dogmatic enunciation of the facts of development of the human mind may urge a theorist in the same direction. We may be told of necessary laws of evolution of the faculties, a necessary progression from the concrete to the abstract and from the simple to the complex, until we begin to imagine that the mind of the child would do perfectly well if only the teacher could be persuaded not to interfere at all. Herbert Spencer has put the case as well as possible:—"If it be true that the mind, like the body, has a predetermined course of evolution, if it unfolds spontaneously, if its successive desires for this or that kind of information arise when these are severally required for its nutrition, if there thus exists in itself a prompter to the right species of activity at the right time, why interfere in any way? Why not leave children wholly to the discipline of nature? Why not remain quite passive and let them get knowledge as they best can? Why not be consistent throughout? This is an awkward-looking question. Plausibly implying, as it does, that a system of complete *laissez-faire* is the logical outcome of the doctrines set forth, it seems to furnish a disproof of them by *reductio ad absurdum*. In truth, however, they do not, when rightly understood, commit us to any such untenable position. A glance at the physical analogies will clearly show this. It is a general law of life that, the more complex the organism to be produced, the longer the period during which it is dependent on a parent organism for food and protection. The difference between the minute, rapidly formed, and self-moving spore of a conferva and the slowly developed seed of a tree, with its multiplied envelopes and large stock of nutriment laid by to nourish the germ during its first stages of growth, illustrates this law in its application to the vegetal world. Among animals we may trace it in a series of contrasts from the monad, whose spontaneously-divided halves are as self-sufficing the moment after their separation as was the original whole, up to man, whose offspring not only passes through a protracted gestation, and subsequently long depends on the breast for sustenance, but after that must have its food artificially administered—must, when it has learned to feed itself, continue to have bread, clothing, and shelter provided, and does not acquire the power of complete self-support till a time varying from fifteen to twenty years after its birth. Now this law applies to the mind as to the body. For mental pabulum also, every higher creature, and especially man, is at first dependent on adult aid. Lacking the ability to move about, the babe is almost as powerless to get materials on which to exercise its perceptions as it is to get supplies for its stomach. Unable to prepare its own food, it is in like manner unable to reduce many kinds of knowledge to a fit form for assimilation. The language through which all higher truths are to be gained it wholly derives from those surrounding it. And we see in such an example as the Wild Boy of Aveyron the arrest of development that results when no help is received from parents and nurses. Thus, in providing from day to day the right kind of facts, prepared in the right manner, and giving them in due abundance at appropriate intervals, there is as much scope for active ministration to a child's mind as to its body. In either case, it is the chief function of parents to see that the conditions requisite to growth are maintained. And as, in supplying aliment and clothing and shelter, they may fulfil this function without at all interfering with the spontaneous development of the limbs and viscera, either in their order or mode, so they may supply sounds for imitation, objects for examination, books for reading, problems for solution, and, if they use neither direct nor indirect coercion, may do this without in any way disturbing the normal process of mental evolution, or rather, may greatly facilitate that process. Hence the admission of the doctrines enunciated, does not, as some might argue, involve the abandonment of teaching, but leaves ample room for an active and elaborate course of culture."[1]

We are, I believe, to mind the rule, but not mechanically or formally; it is like a rule of health. The child's body, for example, is to be kept warm and well fed, but we are not on that account to refrain from sponging it with cold

[1] *Education*, page 67.

water, nor are we to give it food whenever it begins to grow hungry.

We shall draw from our rule such practical maxims as these: Not to encumber with help; not to keep the child's mind passive, while the teacher's mind is working busily; not to use mechanical ways of teaching.

When the children have been cutting out paper, or putting sticks together, the teacher will not say: "That side is too long or too short." He will point out that there is something wrong, and encourage the child to discover what it is. When a model is to be drawn, he will not begin by prescribing the size of the drawing, but will inquire, together with the child, whether the first attempt is convenient in point of size.

Learning by doing follows the same rule. The child begins confidently, not seeing any difficulty; then makes a mistake or is stopped by want of skill. The teacher helps the child to discover the mistake, and to get over the difficulty, but does not warn against possible blunders, unless there is risk of serious disaster.

In the object-lesson the children will be asked to point out the facts of structure, and, if untrained, they will very likely omit all the most important. The teacher will not instantly remedy the defect, but will bring it home by-and-by. Perhaps the skin and the stalk and the pips of the apple have been left out. Questions about the living apple will discover these omissions, and make it clear how impossible it is for the apple to exist without things which have been forgotten.

We shall not be formal or proceed always by one road, lest we deaden the child's interest, on which all the rest depends. A long enumeration of facts, a long exercise in inference or interpretation, a long practical exercise, all these are wearisome to a young child. A good lesson will have something of each, but not very much. A knowing teacher will venture now and then to digress and give an unexpected turn to the lesson in order to revive the interest. We begin with the shape of a leaf of duckweed, and by-and-by, to our surprise, we are experimenting on the surface-tension of water. But the good teacher will come back to his duckweed in the end, and will never have really left it.

The hand of the teacher will guide the lesson throughout, little as the class may be aware of it. It is he who gently presses a vital question, and discourages a foolish one. But, if the children are both able and willing to take even a step or two for themselves, the teacher will gladly give them the chance. There are educational theorists who would leave the guidance, too, in the hands of the children. For my own part, I do not accept their system, but wait until I come to know the wise and capable men and women who have been produced by it. I cannot understand a gospel of Nature which leaves children to bring themselves up.

"Finding out" must not be interpreted so loosely as to include looking up words in a dictionary, or other tasks of the same kind. It is only when the finding out gives exercise to the higher faculties that it becomes precious. If I were teaching a language I would tell the class the words which they did not know, and try to tell them something about each word which would make it stick in their memories. I have looked up thousands of words in six or seven languages, and am so far from feeling any satisfaction in my labours that I would spare myself and others as much of this dull mechanical business as could possibly be contrived. Looking up words in a dictionary is no more profitable than consulting an index of any other sort; when we have it to do, let us go through it cheerfully, but the less of it the better. We need never be anxious to find drudging work for our pupils; they will get enough of that in any serious occupation, and the teacher should take all pains to keep it down.

The good teacher will observe his own progress as well as the progress of the children. The further he goes in the right path the more possible will he find it to mind the rule, "Never to tell the child what he can find out for himself." And the rule, not kept slavishly or literally, will at length become the main guide of his teaching. He will think of it more constantly, and respect it more sincerely, than any other.

PLAIN SPEECH.

I suppose that any sensible person who has to teach science to young persons will be careful to use as few as possible of the long-tailed words of Greek and Latin origin which abound in technical treatises. They cannot be avoided altogether, but we can do without a good many even of those in common use. It is quite a mistake to suppose that the learned language of the books necessarily contributes to precision. On the contrary, the best way of testing the precision of your exposition is to put it into the very simplest language. Many a logical error, many a defect of knowledge is consciously or unconsciously buried in learned words. A certain naturalist, whose writings it has been my illluck now and then to consult, gets over all his difficulties of fact by the help of an English-Latin dictionary. When he really does not know what an organ is, he plies his dictionary, and presents you with a new term.

It is surprising to find how many of the words

which bother youngsters can be translated into the vernacular. I am more and more convinced that nearly everything which we have to explain to boys and girls under sixteen can be explained in homely English words. The habit of mind which leads a man to favour simplicity in language is valuable to every scientific student. You want him to give a straightforward account of what he has seen and done. Encourage him then to study simplicity in speech, not to use Latin or Greek if English will do, not to tag his sentences with ornamental quotations—to disregard that fear of bringing in the same word in successive lines which is the bane of writers who would be thought elegant.

> Si vous voulez dire: Il pleut, dites: Il pleut.
> —*La Bruyère.*

The use of plain language, strong where strength is needed, but always direct and homely, is of importance as a help to simplicity of character. The man who in externals is always practising trivial deceptions, who pretends to wear more clean linen than he really does, who pretends to possess furniture of costly woods while he really can afford nothing better than stained deal, is all the more disposed to pretend to have discovered, when he is merely guessing.

The teacher of English composition bids you avoid a close repetition of a noun or verb. When it comes in a second time in two or three lines you are to substitute another noun or verb. This particular instruction is responsible for much of the obscurity and triviality of our writing. The variety of phrase disguises even from the writer himself the fact that he is saying the same thing over and over again. I take a choice specimen of this flower of style from a newspaper of April, 1894. Observe the writer's anxiety to avoid the repetition of such words as *dog*, *hospice*, and *child*, and see what comes of it.

> The famous dogs of the Hospice of the Great St. Bernard are said to be degenerating. We are told by a lady who recently visited that establishment that there are now only five animals of the old stock remaining. Lovers of the canine race will be sorry if the ancient monastic pile should ultimately lose its breed of remarkable quadrupeds, with which so many narratives of our childhood are inseparably blended. It would be nothing short of a public calamity if the four-footed friend of the traveller lost in the snow should finally disappear from the list of our domesticated animals. Even though they may become extinct as a race, the benevolent and faithful brutes, so long associated with that picturesque shelter amid the Alpine snows, will survive in the affections of youth, and in the story-books of the younger members of every family.

Really eminent writers have, at times, sacrificed to this frivolous rule. Macaulay, who knew so well what is gained by brevity and directness, was capable now and then of writing in such manner as this: "Bishop Compton was the agent employed to manage the clergy; Admiral Herbert undertook to exert all his influence over the navy; and an interest was established in the army by the instrumentality of Churchill."

If the reader should by chance have practised wood-carving, he will know what I mean if I compare the accepted rules of English composition to sandpaper. The free use of sandpaper smooths away irregularities and mistakes; it also makes the work totally uninteresting.

Reporters should look to their English. Such phrases as "vehicular traffic was completely suspended" are intolerable. Common vulgarisms are: *gentleman* for *man*, *residence* for *house*, *communicate intelligence* for *tell*, *effect a landing* for *land*, *casualty* for *accident*, *fatality* for *death*, *period* for *time*.[1]

The best English writers say: "The sun shines *bright*" (not *brightly*). Metaphorical expressions often betray a habit of exaggeration in the writer. "The tables literally groaned," etc. The metaphor is violent enough if we leave out *literally*. "At least, on the lowest possible estimate," etc., are dangerous words to a careless writer, because they slip in when he is not attending.

[1] A period recurs. *Circuit, cycle,* and *orbit* are pretty close synonyms.

The bad writer loves force when he can get it cheap.

Among small faults I may mention over-punctuation. Inverted commas for instance are used profusely, whether they serve a useful purpose or not. It is often wearisome to the reader to be reminded that a trivial phrase has been used before. But now and then it is the printer and not the writer who should be scolded. I can seldom keep the compositor to the modest allowance of stops which really helps the reader.

Since English prose began to be written in plenty there has been a succession, pretty well unbroken, of authors who wrote as they talked, who made distinctness and brevity their first aim. Roger Ascham, Hugh Latimer, North (of North's Plutarch), Dryden, South, Bunyan, Addison, Swift, Defoe, Johnson, Sterne, and Scott, all write in this manner at times, though they may be led away by some prevalent affectation in their unlucky moments. If ever the directness of English prose was seriously threatened, it was by the allusive, conventionally elegant Latinism of Robertson and Gibbon, which has left a smear on much of the writing of the last and the present century. That style is now the mark of the least educated and worst bred—may it never come into favour again!

If you have to write, write in such a way that your faults show themselves. Suppose that there is emptiness, needless repetition, contradiction, confusion of thought, bad reasoning: they will appear, if you write simply. Let them appear. Do not hide them, but clear them away. Love plainness of speech; it will save you from many mistakes, and give you access to many minds.

SCHOOL HOURS.

Good lessons are few, and bad lessons many. The teacher perhaps comes unprepared, and the class weary; then they all toil through the hour like a caravan in loose sand. There is no thought in the lesson, nothing for the children's minds to dwell upon, only stodgy facts and tiresome routine.

Good lessons are costly. They tax both teacher and class; they demand time and skill and money. No pressure of school-managers, trying to equalize an over-loaded budget, can succeed in making good lessons cheap until the market is crowded with well-instructed and well-trained teachers to a degree of which we at present see no sign.

Let us suppose that in a particular school the conditions are more favourable than common, the teacher capable, the class intelligent. Will not the lesson be profitable? Hardly, unless weariness has been provided against. The class-room must be airy, children and teacher alike unexhausted. Even when these precautions have been taken, we must be sure that the lesson is ready, turned over afresh in the teacher's mind, and cast into a shape suitable for that very class.

In colleges we think two lectures a day a good deal. There are experiments to arrange, diagrams or lantern-slides to provide, books to read, notes to make. There is also the unceasing flow of petty business, which ruins study and turns hours into minutes. Moreover, the professor or lecturer has to do something for his subject. He must now and then break through the crust of familiar knowledge; and draw up his own bucketful of new stuff. His class will not do their part unless they are led by a man who has proved his mettle. The more advanced students like to see their professor's name now and then in a title-page or in a foot-note. Hence a professor who means to make his mark devotes a large part of those vacations which seem at first sight so exorbitant to special studies. Advanced students do the same, and a college vacation is to many of them a particularly profitable season.

In the school we can dispense with the published memoirs as proof of the teacher's competence. The form master or mistress need not be oppressed by interviews and correspondence, but experiments and special illustrations are still wanted in many subjects, and the lesson nearly always requires leisurely preparation.

Some subjects require much preparation, others little, a few none. A quite elementary lesson in language or arithmetic may be given by an experienced teacher without notice. But the history, literature, science or language lesson of a middle or upper form will soon become poor and dry if the teacher does not prepare for it; seeking apt illustrations of difficult points, interesting passages to quote, new problems to set. Besides all this, the teacher will grow rusty if he makes no progress with his own studies. "So long as we humbly learn we may hopefully teach," said Arnold. What if the teacher has not time to learn?

I must try to come to close quarters with this question, even at the risk of being dogmatic. How much can the teacher be expected to do in school with his whole force? The best opinion that I can form is that a teacher of average power cannot be looked to for more than two lessons a day of the more taxing sort—lessons, I mean, which call forth varied powers without break or remission. A lesson in geometry, or French, or arithmetic, should as a rule be of this kind, giving the teacher no pause at all, but keeping him on the strain the whole way through. Two such lessons should not come together. If they are of right quality and right intensity, neither teacher nor class can keep them up long. An hour of rest or of slighter exertion should be interposed.

A lesson should not exceed the academical hour of fifty minutes, and should be shorter than this in junior forms. The unspent balance is wanted for changing class-rooms, opening windows, and running in the fresh air.

When the teacher has given his two set lessons with full vigour, not sparing himself in the least, he need not be completely spent. There are lighter duties for which he is still perfectly fit, and among these is supervision of various things which the class can do almost by themselves. Map-drawing, letter-writing in English, French, or German, essay-writing, answering questions on paper, working problems on paper, the dictation of a low form, the unseen translation of a higher form,—all these are examples of class-work which does not try the teacher very severely. I need hardly say that the boys and girls ought to be considered even more tenderly, and the first question with respect to a new time-table should be whether there is alternation of hard and easy, with frequent and sufficient intervals of play or rest.

Exercises and correction of exercises are the

bane of teachers and scholars alike. The common sense of the business is that the inevitable mistakes should be corrected almost as soon as they are perpetrated. Once allow them to sink into the boy's mind, and they are at least as likely to root themselves there as the tardy and unimpressive corrections. Some schoolmasters will at all hazards make their corrections felt. "Write out all these grammatical corrections a hundred times," is the gross, unfair, and mechanical remedy. But injustice does not prosper long. The schoolboy requites such teaching as that with sullen indifference to the subject.

What the scholars may be trusted to do for themselves is the repetition of processes which have been thoroughly explained to them. Give them practice in doing things which they completely understand, and their mistakes or shortcomings will not be deadly. On no account should all difficulties be swept out of their path. But let the difficulties come up naturally and spontaneously, or, if deliberately set before the class, let them be carefully selected as appropriate to their faculties and present attainments. To give a boy a book crammed with difficulties of Latin syntax got together by an ingenious exercise-writer, and to force him to work through it in his evenings and under penalties, is a crudity worthy of the age of chipped stone implements.

If the more taxing lessons are reduced in number and well spaced, the teacher can continue them day after day without excessive fatigue. Call upon him to take four or five severe lessons in almost close succession, and then to correct exercises for an hour or two in the evening, and you may perhaps get your tale of bricks. But spirit, cheerfulness and force, interest in the subject, novel illustrations, improvement in method, sympathy with the children—these most assuredly you will not get.

A teacher who is in earnest will not be satisfied unless his class is pretty frequently set down to work by themselves. He will judge by their work how far they are profiting by his instructions. Hence, though we must condemn the written grammatical exercise, if it brings up new rules which have never been explained, and is only corrected after an interval of a day or two, the class may and should work on paper without close supervision. What they do should be corrected in school time, and after an interval not exceeding a very few hours. Do not trench upon the teacher's hours of recreation and study.

Two hours of vigorous teaching, two or three hours of lighter school-work, with which a moderate amount of correction may be combined, and two hours of preparation for the next day, is enough for any teacher. Wherever it is possible he should have the use of a room at school with books and other appliances for study, and take no atom of school-business home.

When I plead for shorter hours for the children and shorter hours for the teacher, I may expect general approval, unless, indeed, surly councils and committees and boards demur to these pleasant reforms. But my next proposal will not be nearly so popular. The vacations of secondary schools seem to me unreasonably long. Six or seven weeks in summer, a month at Christmas, and three weeks at Easter or Whitsuntide I consider to be absurd. Holidays of such length are not profitable or even enjoyable, and nothing can excuse them except the unreasonable strain of the school term. I should concede just so many weeks in summer as are required for the customary holiday of the parents. A clear month seems to me ample. A fortnight at Christmas and a week in the spring would suffice for minor vacations.

In fact unlimited enjoyment is by no means my programme. Efficiency on human conditions is what I seek to promote, and efficiency is never to be had without toil. Idleness—so many weeks of loafing, or lawn-tennis, or fireside pipes, or cricket—is no more necessary to the schoolmaster and his boys than to the man of business and the factory-worker.

Equalization rather than reduction of school-hours is therefore my plan. It is only in junior forms that I would have the total time spent in school materially curtailed. But I would get rid of most of the home-work of higher forms, and of all the home-work of junior forms. It is untidy, and half-understood; it spoils home diversions and home education; it is not so much an aid to good teaching as a substitute for good teaching. Let the schoolmaster and the younger schoolboys, at least, finish their work at school, and go home with light hearts and good consciences.

HOW TO MAKE ROOM FOR ALL THE SUBJECTS WHICH ARE TO BE TAUGHT IN SCHOOLS.

If the schoolmaster were very teachable, what a time he would have! No one can write on education without insisting on new subjects, and yet the old claims are not relaxed. We must have natural science in several branches, modern languages (more efficient than heretofore), drawing, and gymnastics. But classics, and mathematics, and divinity, and cricket, and football, must be kept up or even improved.

Increased hours are not to be thought of; indeed many people think that the school-hours are already too long. Fewer lessons, shorter lessons, and not so much home-work are the cry. More potatoes to carry, and a smaller basket to put them in. We may well wish the schoolmaster strength to take a line of his own.

I believe that the problem is not an insoluble one after all. All that is essential can, I think, be got into something less than the customary time. But, to manage this, we have to begin gently, and to bring the boy over to our side; that means study of his nature, and adaptation of our methods to his strength and weaknesses.

I will not in this paper propose a single important change which has not been actually tried with good results. It would be pure waste of time to describe methods which have never been put into practice. Nor will I speak of methods which have never been tried on large classes and under school-conditions. Many of the suggestions here made are drawn from the settled practice of foreign schools, and are unfamiliar to English teachers merely because we have so little curiosity about what our neighbours are doing.

Suppose that at eight years of age the boy passes out of the preparatory school and begins book-learning. Take a good look at him before you start, and notice his curly head, his "shining morning face," his restless hands and feet. I want you to realize that he is an absolute child still. He has curiosity and activity; he is quick to imitate grown-up people. But he has little perseverance; he cannot sit still long together; he cannot think continuously. Such a child must learn a little at a time. He must learn from spoken words rather than from printed books. He must have plenty of easy, varied, childish occupations, which exercise hand, and foot, and tongue. Don't forget that he has many things to do beside his lessons. He has to grow, to play, to prosecute a thousand private activities. His imagination is likely to be strong; his notions of accuracy and duty weak.

Watch him at his games. See how ready he is to combine and organize, how quick to imitate real life.

These qualities of the boy are your opportunities or your obstacles according to the way in which you treat them. Try to screw him down to the Latin grammar. He will resist or evade you. If at last you carry your point, it will only be by weakening his natural force, and treating him as a conquered enemy. Try to interest him in a piece of real and necessary work. He is willing, but awkward, and soon tires. He is good for little as yet—a colt, that will be ruined if you harness him to the cart before he is fit for it. If you are content to work him gently for a time, to begin with the things that he likes and is curious about, you may do much with him in the end.

But if you are zealous and impatient, you may do him much harm; you cannot possibly do him any good.

There are two or three things which the boy of eight will take to with alacrity. He will gladly learn to draw. Give him paper and pencil and a colour-box, and let him copy the shapes of various coloured objects. Among other things let him trace and paint the countries of Europe and the counties of England. Attend carefully to the way in which he does his work, and see that he gets hold of the best methods. Teach him to get the shapes true, to lay his colours evenly, to letter neatly. But do not trouble him to learn the names by heart. You will find before long that without word said he has learned all the names which signify.

Now is the time to teach him the rudiments of a foreign tongue. You will naturally choose a spoken tongue, and French is on many accounts the best for your purpose. You want no books at all in this stage. Begin with the names of the objects about you. Teach your class the French names of the things in the room, the things in their pockets, and so on. You can go a good way with only two verbs, *avoir* and *être*. Let the others slip in one at a time. When you have had your five or ten minutes' conversation, let the boys write down a few simple sentences from dictation.

Stories from English history will be welcome. Tell them in your own words, instead of reading them or hearing them read. Show pictures by the lantern of the boats and houses of the time, photographs of the old castles and abbeys. Draw rough maps on the blackboard, and get the children to make better maps for the next lesson. Every story will furnish a short dictation. Story, ten minutes; dictation and correction, ten minutes; questions, ten minutes. Half-an-hour for the whole lesson will be enough at first.

Arithmetic and the simplest elements of geometry will require another daily lesson. Do not make your arithmetic too rational, but bring out its practical uses as much as you can. In the geometry you want to illustrate rather than prove. There need be no demonstrations as yet.

Reading aloud will enter into every day's work. Clear pronunciation is to be attended to from the first, and it costs much trouble to get it. Little pieces of poetry may be learned by heart. It is a good plan to divide a poem into stanzas or short lengths, and let each child read the same portion aloud every day. After four or five days he knows his own portion. After four or five recitals without book, he knows every other boy's portion too.

It is well not to take two sitting lessons in succession. After half-an-hour's French or arithmetic, let the children be drilled in the open air, or dance, or practice jumping.

Continue a little longer the various arts already learned in the kindergarten. Compasses, and a T-square, and an inch measure may be used now and then. Give the class little geometrical problems, such as to describe a circle about a square, to make a parallelogram equal to a given triangle.

Once or twice a week a letter should be written. It will be done ever so much better if it is to be posted when written and addressed.

There need be no separate lessons in writing, spelling, dictation, or grammar. These will enter into every lesson in English history, French, etc.

The geography and English history will gradually become more formal. But I would never use a text-book of geography at all, and I would never give a lesson out of a school history. It can be used now and then as a book of reference. Train the children little by little to turn up in the history the particular facts which are wanted for the class lesson.

At nine or ten the reading of an easy French book may be undertaken. One copy of the book in the teacher's hand is enough. A tale-book is to be preferred, and there is nothing better than a tale by Erckmann-Chatrian. Read a short passage aloud in French. Have it translated clause by clause. Dictate it to the class, and correct the dictations on the spot. Give short explanations and frequent questions on points of grammar. Frame sentences in French out of the words contained in the passage just read. Vary these, until the idioms have become perfectly familiar. By this time the regular verbs, and perhaps a few others, will have been learned by heart, bit by bit, and in class.

In arithmetic, there will now be a short blackboard lesson given every day, and half-an-hour's practice on paper or slate.

An object lesson may be usefully given once or twice a week. Drilling, or dancing, and drawing, should be kept up steadily.

The lessons are gradually lengthened to fifty minutes, the last ten minutes of the hour being occupied by changing class-rooms and running out in the open air. Three lessons a day are enough for boys of ten, but lighter occupations will fill up another hour or two of their time. Two lessons requiring close attention should come together as seldom as possible.

At twelve years of age there is still no striking change; there are three regular lessons a day, viz.: English, French, and arithmetic with geometry. Two object lessons in natural history and one in experimental science may be given in the course of the week. Map drawing, model drawing, drilling, and gymnastics fill up the rest of the school time. No home-work is required as yet.

At fourteen, a second language, Latin or German, may be introduced, and French will claim less time. If it has been well taught, the class will now be able to read, write, and speak French with tolerable ease. Continual practice and revision of the grammar are, of course, still required. Natural history may now be left to the school club, and experimental science may receive more serious attention. There will be four set lessons a day, a number which should not be exceeded without careful consideration. I suppose that two of these are specially prepared by the teacher, the other two less taxing.

The exercises should be short and *extempore*, given out and corrected in class. It is useless for the boys to write at great length exercises which are not corrected till the next day or the day after. After so long an interval the mistakes have as good a chance of being remembered as anything else.

I should not be inclined to spend much time upon English grammar. The boy who knows any other grammar need only take up English grammar as a special subject. Treated historically, it can be made very delightful, as may many other special subjects, but we need not put it among the indispensables. Some of the text-books which treat of English grammar and analysis of sentences make me bless my own stupid old school, which never mentioned these things at all. Mastery of English, I would remark, does not come by grammar and analysis, but by observation and practice.

Many people, chiefly schoolmasters and arts professors, will object to the introduction of no more than two foreign languages into the school course. And yet any one who collects evidence on the point will soon find out for himself that the average grammar-school boy gets only a miserable smattering of the Latin, Greek, and French which custom requires. When he leaves school, he cannot read, write, speak, or understand one of them. Now I do know, from actual experience, that an hour a day for five or six years will give a boy or girl command of one foreign language, and a useful knowledge of a second. Let us, then, go for two only, and relinquish without regrets the unattainable third. It is the three languages, never really learned, which overburden the school course. We are like the monkeys which clutch at so many nuts that they carry none off.

No doubt there are boys here and there of exceptional literary gifts who would thrive well enough upon a school education largely made up of Latin and Greek. There are also a very few who would thrive upon mathematics or experimental science. But it is neither just nor sensible to make these early specialists the rule for the multitude. The specialists ought to get through the ordinary course betimes, and work at their own subjects for the three or four years which can be saved between the completion of the ordinary school-course (fifteen or sixteen) and matriculation at the University (nineteen). Even for them, early specialization has many risks.

"It is not what is done at school that is so important," I have more than once heard a schoolmaster say, "but what is done afterwards. We sow the seeds at school, which grow up into trees later on. Surely it is a good thing to get through the tiresome rudiments betimes. Grown men and women will not fag at grammar, but they will carry on in after life the studies which they began at school." The practical inference is drawn that we do well to give the schoolboy a slight knowledge of several languages.

There is one thing about this argument which moves me more than it would some other people, and that is the circumstance that I used it myself in all sincerity of conviction a good many years ago. But, unless it is substantiated by facts there is not much in it, and the facts, when you get at them, tell all the other way. I will ask the reader to apply the following test for himself. Put down on a sheet of paper the names of all your male relatives, brothers, uncles, cousins, who have grown to be men, and also the languages of which they have practical mastery. If your experience at all resembles that of the people who have made the trial before, you will find hardly a single case in which there is mastery of three languages, and few in which there is mastery of two. Some will be found to know one modern language well, mostly because of residence abroad. But the commonest case of all is that in which no foreign language, ancient or modern, is possessed. As things go, it is unusual for the lawyer, or doctor, or clergyman, to have mastered any one foreign language to the point at which it can be used in conversation or correspondence. I feel persuaded that it would be a real gain to the culture of the English people if every capable grammar-school boy got sound French, and no foreign language besides.

I would not in the least press the claims of science upon the schoolmaster. Pleasant talks about natural history, and entertaining lessons on the chemistry and physics of every-day life, are usually enough for boys under fourteen. I have found the dreariest stuff taught in schools under the name of science. Chemical analysis, in particular, is nearly always badly done, and, even if it is well done, the schoolboy is not ready for it. The professor of chemistry will tell you that his students are seldom better, and often worse, for the chemistry they did at school.

We want to inoculate the curious schoolboy with scientific ideas, rather than to put him through a systematic course of science. The systematic course will come fitly when he has passed out of the imitative into the reflective stage. The passage is marked by the discontinuance of the imaginative games, in which the boy pretends to be somebody else. Set before your unreflecting schoolboy mechanisms, natural and human contrivances, puzzles and simple problems. Never produce your systems. Take a fresh subject each time. Excite and stimulate his curiosity, for that is the instrument by which you can get the work done. I would have no text-book of science produced in the school, except in the upper classes, and then only for reference.

Young boys should, I think, have no home-work to do. They should have their evenings and holidays free for play, and home reading, and fret-work, and wood-carving, and natural-history rambles. It is the indolence and selfishness of the parents which makes them cry out for home-lessons to keep the children quiet. After fourteen, a moderate quantity of home-work, say an hour a day, will do no harm. But it should never be set upon the new and hard parts of the subject in hand; the good teacher will save these for the class-lesson, and set home-work on the applications of what has been mastered in class. The new bit of translation, the new grammatical construction, the new step in algebra, will be taken in class, but the little historical essay, the illustrative map, or the practical problem in geometry, will be chosen as an exercise to be done out of school. I would give the home-work as much as possible of a voluntary character; it should never be essential to the progress of the schoolboy.

These recommendations as to home-work are largely based upon what I find to answer with the older boys who come to college. We do the essential part of our work in the laboratory and class-room, and do it in such a way that no one can by mere thoughtlessness miss the meaning of what is going on. We have few subjects in hand at once. Five is considered too many, especially if one or two are new. The work done out of college (I am speaking here mainly of the biological work) is voluntary, and intended to excite interest or ensure practical mastery rather than to cover part of the teaching routine.

Why should the half-trained youngster be treated with less consideration than the older student; have his subjects multiplied, and the hard parts left to be puzzled out at home?

I would beg the schoolmaster who finds himself unable to cope with a crowded time-table to simplify the business at all hazards. Take up only so many subjects that each may come round pretty nearly every day. Limit the lessons to fifty minutes (less in junior forms), and have ten minutes out of every hour for a scamper out of doors. Let the home-work sink to a subsidiary, and in great part voluntary, occupation for the older and more ambitious boys. Above all, trust to enlightened and animated teaching, and not to long hours and the fear of punishment.

THE TEACHING OF SUBJECTS AND THE TEACHING OF SCHOLARS.

D. A well-to-do Drysalter.
S. A Schoolmaster.

D. I have called this evening to consult you about my boy, Sam. He is just eight years old, and I think it is time he began to do something useful.

S. What has he been doing so far?

D. His mother would have him sent to Miss B.'s kindergarten. I don't think much of the kindergarten system myself: there is so much about gifts and coloured wools and strips of paper, which cannot be of any real good, you know. I call it nothing but play.

S. Happily there is no great hurry; your son is only eight years old.

D. Yes, but I want to make a beginning as soon as I can. We ought not to waste these early years, or we shall feel the difference later on.

S. Certainly, we ought not to waste time. But I should be quite satisfied if a boy of eight had made a promising start.

D. That is just it! I want to make a promising start. My boy, I may tell you, is going to be a drysalter like myself.

S. It seems early to take his future calling into account, if the boy is only eight.

D. No doubt; but I want to consider the end from the beginning. I want my boy to learn nothing useless.

S. The less the better. But we cannot specialize with a boy of eight.

D. What do you mean by specializing?

S. Taking a special line.

D. That's the very thing I want Sam to do from the first.

S. Happily, you are not obliged to put him to work early; it will be soon enough to consider his preparation for business when he is several years older.

D. I don't agree with you. The sooner he begins to prepare for business the better. I don't want him to learn Latin and things of that sort.

S. But I suppose that you want to give him a really good education?

D. It depends upon what you mean by a really good education. I want the boy to be smart at accounts, and to write a good hand, and to have a good style about him. I should like him to know a bit of chemistry too. Chemistry is of use in our business—there is so much humbug to contend with; people try to sell you inferior stuff, and you must know all about the things you have to buy.

S. We can do something for his chemistry later on; but there are things which have to come first which are quite as important as accounts and chemistry.

D. What are they?

S. Well, you want him to love work, I suppose

D. So I do, and I find that at present he is much fonder of play.

S. It is natural and right that a boy of eight should be much fonder of play than of work. But he should be beginning to like work as well.

D. What can you do to make a boy fond of work?

S. Interest him in it. If you set him down, whatever he may be thinking of, and make him work sums for you, he will probably hate the sums. We ought to begin by interesting him in figures.

D. A capital thing if you can manage it; but it

is not very easy to interest boys in sums and figures.

S. It can be done. I often take a class of small boys, and get them to play at keeping shop. They weigh out what they call groceries, and keep accounts, and send out their bills. They soon catch the idea, and their imaginations supply all deficiencies. We weigh sand instead of raisins or sugar, but the scales and weights are real ones, and the bills are added up correctly. This is a very popular game.[1] Rather older boys are made to work out the cost of a new cricket pavilion. They have to mention all the articles required, and to fix likely prices for them; then they find the total cost, and the total sum of the subscriptions in hand to pay it. There is perhaps a deficiency, on which the bank charges interest, which has to be reckoned. We teach a good deal in this way. Sometimes a question is put which requires measurement; for instance, how many square yards are there in the schoolroom? How many cubic yards? What is the height of the vane on the school tower?—which cannot be measured directly. All these give excellent practice. We don't teach arithmetic in this way alone, but these practical questions are the life and soul of the teaching.

[1] Boxes of cardboard coins, suitable for practical Arithmetic, can be bought of E. J. Arnold & Son, Leeds.

D. I like that kind of teaching very well. But do you mean to say that Sam could find out the height of the vane by himself?

S. Not yet. But he could weigh out sand into paper bags, and keep the accounts of imaginary customers in shillings and pence. We often set the boys to find out the capacity of large glass or tin-plate vessels of various shapes, such as globes, cylinders, and funnels. Some very pretty calculations are required to get right answers. Afterwards the calculations are checked by filling the vessels with water and measuring the water.

D. That looks interesting too. It would be very useful afterwards to an exciseman or an oil-merchant.

S. Or any one else. It would be useful to any boy to be able to measure the oil in a cask, with nothing but a tape, because he must have learnt so many things before he can get so far as that. He must, among the rest, have learnt how to measure correctly, and you would be surprised to find how few people can be trusted to do that. But the thing which we have chiefly at heart is to make the boys love work, to be fond of doing things, whether they are required to do them or not, and to hate idleness.

D. That is capital if you can only manage it.

S. It can generally be done if a boy has any curiosity about things. Curiosity and imagination are the motive power of our school. We try to make the boys want to know, and then help them to find out. And imagination is the chief incentive to curiosity. You must not be surprised if we work at certain subjects merely because they exercise a boy's imagination and excite his curiosity.

D. I think there may be some risk of a boy's imagination running away with him. We don't want imagination in the counting-house.

S. It is the dreaming imagination which is dangerous. There is no fear of the power of imagination being abused if the things imagined have immediately to be done. Imagination is in its right place as an incentive to work.

D. I admit that it is of great consequence that the boy should work with a will at whatever he has in hand. When do you think he ought to begin chemistry?

S. Not just yet. A science, to be followed out methodically, requires much greater steadiness and power of thought than a young boy can be expected to possess. It is rare to find even a well-educated boy who is really fit to study chemistry before fourteen.

D. I should not have thought it necessary to wait so long.

S. Chemistry, like any other science, requires a power of continuous thought which no entirely immature mind can give. We like to train a schoolboy upon things which can be studied a little at a time. When the judgment is stronger, and the boy or man can appreciate evidence, the time has come to study a science systematically. Meanwhile, I should not leave the boy quite ignorant either of scientific facts or scientific principles. But I should introduce them a few at once, and give him plenty of time to make them his own. The child thinks, and sometimes thinks intently, but never for long together. His attention soon tires. For that reason our lower classes now change lessons every half-hour. Leave us to train your boy for a few years in our own way. We will interest him in work, and gradually show him how to apply his mind to a new subject, or to get the right conclusion from a number of particulars. When he has been well practised in all this by doing it every day for years together, we will start him with chemistry and you will find that no time has been lost.

D. I should have thought that the little bit of chemistry we require could be picked up without so much training of the mind.

S. Mr. D., you know a good deal about horses, and very likely you know a good deal about the breaking-in of horses. To train a young horse to run quietly in harness takes much time and patience. It is a far harder thing to train a man's mind, because the finished product is so much higher. Don't be surprised if it cost years to accomplish it. There are habits to form, as well as knowledge to impart. We take a young child of small physical strength, with many desires and fears, impatient and restless, and we want to train that child into a strong man, able to control his desires and fears, able to think long and hard, able to endure hardship and toil for the sake of a remote benefit. The boy has not only to be trained, but to grow. Getting knowledge is the least part of the business. Among other things your boy has to live with others. You would like him to be a popular young fellow, interesting to those whom he meets every day.

D. Certainly I should; but I have not found that it makes much difference to all that what school you have been to.

S. The natural disposition of the boy and his home influences tell much more than the things which he does at school, I admit. But it is something for a young fellow to be prepared to take his share in social occupations and amusements. Dancing and part-singing are excellent for this reason, and those young men and women who cannot take any part in them are at some disadvantage.

D. No doubt, but, after all, these are small matters. The main thing is to make sure that the young man can earn his daily bread.

S. Whatever encourages young people to co-operate for a common purpose is likely to be of use. I would have a boy prepared by school and college to take an interest in other people's cares, and to help in public business.

D. Very good, if he does not mind other people's affairs to the neglect of his own.

S. Don't force your son to stand aside when an interesting conversation or discussion is going on, merely because he has not the common knowledge of history or English literature which is required. He has to make himself interesting to others, and one way of securing that end is to give him pursuits which others will be likely to share. Don't let your boy be quite incapable of taking part in a political meeting or a conversation club, because he knows about nothing except accounts and chemistry and his own business.

D. He must go on improving after he has left school. All that I can do is to start him.

S. That is all that any one can do. But give him an effective start, and don't oblige him to learn as a man the things which can be easily and pleasantly learnt as a boy.

D. There is no end to that kind of preparation

for elegant conversation. Perhaps you would advise me to send my boy to college, and let him go into the counting-house at two or three and twenty.

S. I can't see so far ahead. Let us go on gently, and decide for at most a year or two in advance. As a general rule, I don't think a man of business should go to the University, if it means putting off his entrance upon active business to so late an age as two or three and twenty. An excellent education can be given if he goes into the mill or counting-house at eighteen or nineteen. As you said just now, he can go on improving. I should like to give him such a start that he can go on improving for the rest of his life.

D. That seems a good deal. Are you pretty sure that you can manage all that you can undertake?

S. I perhaps undertake less than you suppose. I undertake to try my best. We often fail in this or that particular because we are wanting in sense and experience and ability. Sometimes we fail for want of energy or talent in the scholar. What I ask of you is that you should not condemn us to failure for want of time.

D. I should be sorry to spoil a promising experiment for the sake of saving a little time. Let us watch the result and see how the boy gets on. But I should like to know a little more about the subjects you would take up. It seems to me so important that we should make a really good choice. I want to get in as many as possible of the things which he will put to use later on, and leave out pretty nearly everything that he will not find useful.

S. I will ask you to give me your confidence instead of stipulating exactly what I am to teach. When I was ten years younger, I attached immense importance to the choice of subjects. It seemed to me the chief thing in education to consider how many languages I should teach, and what languages, how many sciences, and what sciences. Then I would study the preliminaries necessary to these languages and sciences, and I really thought, at one time, that I could give good reasons for adopting a particular curriculum on which I had spent much time and pains. But ten years of additional observation and practice, added to the fact that I have now three boys of my own, have changed my views a good deal. I don't care nearly so much about subjects now, and I care a great deal more about boys. If your little Sam is like most other boys of eight, he will be full of activity, which is often without any definite purpose, and may be called restlessness. He will have plenty of curiosity about things and people. He will be fond of imitating others, and especially of imitating grown-up people.

He will have a lively imagination, and will easily picture himself, after a way of his own, in very novel positions. His imagination will appear most conspicuously in his play, and he will readily suppose himself to be a policeman or a wild Indian. Lastly, he will be social. It will greatly increase his delight if he has school-fellows to share his activity, and his imitations, and his imaginative fancies. His social needs will make the ridicule of his fellows the bitterest of troubles. I should like to turn all these qualities to account, and use them to bring on gently and naturally greater steadiness, method, and reflection. To check him at every turn because he shows the qualities proper to his age would be absurd and mischievous. How are we to use the gifts of childhood? We must use his curiosity by gradually changing it into the thirst for knowledge. We must add perseverance and method to his restless activity. We must employ his love of imitation to gain facility in speech and writing and drawing. We must use his imaginative power as a means of making real to him distant places and people long ago dead. We must strengthen his social instincts, and gradually make them reasonable and permanent. All this is much harder to accomplish than it sounds. It would be easier to confine our attention to subjects, and let the boy's mind take care of itself. But to aid, instead of discouraging, the natural development of the boy's mind is the great problem, and the schoolmaster will not do his duty if he shirks it. You must do your part too. We ask you to be considerate and patient, not to expect rapid changes, not to be disgusted if the boy does not become all that you could wish in the course of a few months. We ask you to expect nothing finished or complete from the boy so long as he is a boy. He is changing day by day, and the one thing to dread beyond almost everything else is that he should stop developing, and begin to take satisfaction in what he is and what he has done. Let him enjoy life, and grow unconsciously. Unconscious development, without much foresight or recollection, is perhaps best for him. It will be years before you or any one can tell what will come of it all. Do not judge our work by subjects, and do not judge our work as if your boy of eight or nine were already in his father's counting-house. We are making preparation for the future, and it is only in the future that the result will appear.

D. It all sounds very well, but I am not sure that I understand above half of it. How can you train the boys so carefully when there are perhaps twenty of them in one class?

S. In some ways it is a disadvantage to teach so many together. We cannot go out of our way for the sake of a particular boy. But by daily observation we get a very fair notion of each boy's progress and requirements. And you must remember that private teaching has its drawbacks too. Boys are social creatures, and they help one another as much in school-work as in play. The best part of our teaching could not be attempted with single children.

D. You throw overboard all my notions of sensible, practical teaching. I could judge for myself whether Sam was shaping right for business. But how am I to tell whether his mind is developing or not, and whether his imagination is being exercised? Sam's imagination, indeed! I am quite sure that you don't know what the boy is like.

S. It is quite natural that you should want to satisfy yourself that your boy is making real progress, and my little experiments cannot prosper as I should like unless we are helped by the parents. Let me ask you simply to observe for the first few months. See whether the boy brings out his drawings and his maps on wet half-holidays or Sunday afternoons. See whether he talks about his problems in arithmetic or geometry at meal-times. Observe him quietly, but don't say much. Don't praise him much, and don't be too ready to find fault or correct. We want him to do things his own way a good deal. Now and then a little friendly interest in his occupations will do good. For instance, when he has done a neat map you might give him a new paint-box. But don't lead the boy to expect admiration, and don't dishearten him by criticism. You can tell very well by a boy's talk whether his mind is growing in the right way or not. Notice whether he talks more sensibly than he did, whether he is interested more and more in real and important subjects. A boy of eight should be dropping babyish talk, empty jokes about absolute trifles, and all that. He should be full of his occupations, whether work or play. He should have his eyes well open, and grow quick to notice things which he has hitherto passed by as beyond him. His letters will give you excellent information. I don't mean so much in the way of improved writing and spelling, as in the choice and handling of subjects. He ought, if his school is doing well for him, to write more sensibly and fully than he used to do, and have a better notion of interesting his correspondent. The most unfavourable sign is apathy and indolence. If he lounges about with his hands in his pockets doing nothing, either play or work, and if this goes on, week after week, I should be the first to recommend you to try some other plan.

D. He won't do that. He's an active little fellow, though not too fond of books. .

S. If he is naturally active we shall do well

enough. Some boys who are naturally indolent can be helped to exert themselves. There are a few who don't answer to the spur at all, and they are very hard to deal with. I suspect they are often in poor health, or else come from homes where nothing interesting ever goes on.

D. Then, so long as the boy is fairly busy, you don't care very much what he is doing?

S. That is as far as possible from my method. I do care immensely what he is doing. I want him to do those things which will develop his powers in a natural way. It is true that I don't care much about the immediate results. A boy of nine or ten can do very little of anything that signifies. Perhaps he may be able to frighten birds out of the corn with a rattle, or something of that sort. The great question is, what is he going to be, what will he be able to do at sixteen or seventeen?

D. Well, I am still a good deal in the dark. Suppose we try your plan for a year or two. I shall get to see better what you are driving at.

S. Do, if you please. I wish you would come across now and then to talk over matters with me. I should like to find out things which only a father or mother can tell me. And I should like to explain my plans, bit by bit, so that you can help me to make them useful and practical.

D. You won't make me into a schoolmaster,

whatever pains you take. I have been a drysalter ever since I was fourteen, and I shall never be anything else.

S. No man can be a drysalter and nothing else, any more than he can be a schoolmaster and nothing else.

LECTURING AND TEACHING.

What is the difference between lecturing and teaching? The lecturer is supposed to possess special information on his subject, and to offer this information to his class in the form of a clear and complete statement. The thinking out is done beforehand by the lecturer alone. The student is expected to note down the lecturer's remarks, or such part as seems most necessary, and afterwards to work over his notes, with or without help from books. Teaching should differ from lecturing in that the lesson is not brought to class ready-made, but is developed step by step in concert with the class. The teacher guides, but the class contributes all that it can. Perhaps the antithesis between lecturing and teaching is not quite happy. I will not engage always to use the words in this particular sense, but for my immediate purpose they will do well enough.

After lecturing to elementary classes in biology for several years, I began to be dissatisfied. The practice of regularly inspecting the students' note-books led me to the discovery that the notes were often worthless. Unimportant things took up too much space; the most fundamental things were omitted or inadequately given. Only the best students understood how to take really useful notes. When I was enlightened on this point, I resolved to instruct my classes in note-making. I urged them to set down only the heads of what was said, to do this in ink and during lecture, and to go over their brief notes by way of recapitulation out of class, instead of copying out their hasty pencil notes—a slavish practice adopted by many students whose industry is greater than their judgment.

Here I failed almost completely. My method required thought and prompt decision. It would have been excellent for the men to think much during the lecture and write little, but their irresistible tendency was to write much and think little. Bit by bit I began to alter my own methods, giving less information and requiring more from the class. Question and answer, which I had always practised, became frequent. By degrees my whole method of instruction was changed, if not reversed.

Formerly I used to tell my class what I wished them to know and only questioned them to make sure that they had understood what had been said. Now I began to require them to furnish the facts, and these I put together as they were supplied, or, better still, encouraged the class to put them together. Then I found that the students could not get out of their text-books all that I wanted. It was necessary that they should have recently seen the things for themselves. Instead of the lecture preparing for the laboratory work, the laboratory work was made to come first, and then the concrete facts known to every one could be used in the lecture-room as material out of which, mainly by question and answer, general results were to be got.

The general result in a biological class may take various forms. It may be a *proposition, e.g.*, that a flower is a metamorphosed shoot; or that marine habitat favours larval stages, while fluviatile habitat discourages them. It may be an *explanation*, which in biology generally means pointing out the advantage to the species of the facts of structure. It may be a *scheme*, verbal or pictorial, giving a simplified view of a complex mass of facts. The vertebra, or the crustacean segment and its appendages, may thus be reduced to schemes. Lastly, it may be nothing more than the definition of a word. Such words as "spore," "seed," "flower," "larva," "tissue" give excellent practice. The examples are to be collected and compared, and the definition inferred from them.

The best guide to the laboratory work is not the lecture, but the practical text-book, which is always at the student's elbow, and is arranged with a view to quick reference. The student sees and draws the object, and checks his first conceptions by immediate comparison with it.

The teacher soon finds out that the two methods of lecturing and teaching are fundamentally different. The first difference concerns himself mainly. Lecturing is easy; if you know your subject moderately well and have once made a tolerable selection from the materials at command, you can lecture acceptably by repeating year after year the old statements and the old explanations. Teaching is always hard when you draw your materials in great part from the class. To get useful results from a collection of facts contributed in no particular order by a number of persons means rapid thinking and arrangement. You must have the essential points so clear in your own mind that you cannot be put out, even though your facts are supplied to you upside down. The difference to the class is equally great. On one plan the great thing is to write fast; on the other the great thing is to offer useful facts to the teacher, and to draw just inferences. To both parties it is the difference between a mechanical method, easy but unstimulating, and a living method. With a class of any spirit the live method will, when it is once mastered, be recognized as the better thing. But you have to pay for your advantages; the live method costs both time and trouble.

Lecturing aims at giving information; teaching aims also at discipline. To both teacher and student the way in which the result is got may be far more important than the result itself. In a later stage, discipline becomes less necessary, and special information more valuable. Hence the advanced class can be lectured to with profit. It gets its discipline out of reading and independent laboratory work, or even out of the simpler kinds of research. When two biologists meet, they tell one another things, but they don't offer discipline to one another. The professor and an advanced class should be on something like the same terms.

People warned me beforehand of the difficulty of getting a class to say what they knew; but I have had no serious trouble of this kind. It is well to begin gently, and encourage the students by asking about things which they know perfectly well. In time the better men will explain complicated matters clearly and fluently. I have no doubt that they are much the better for getting rid of sheepishness, and learning to arrange their thoughts and words. It ought to be unnecessary to say that the weaker members of the class should never be shown up in a bad light. Merciless criticism of a stupid answer would discourage half the class and destroy the chances of success. The questioning should not be all on the teacher's side. I encourage my students to ask questions of their own, to stop me when they have not understood perfectly, or are dissatisfied with the conclusion arrived at. The more discussion we get into the lesson, the more, as a rule, the class is interested, provided, of course, that the discussions are on points of real importance. Here, as everywhere, we must avoid triviality. Sometimes I cannot treat a particular biological subject as I should like, but am obliged to resort to bare description. This is occasionally due to the circumstance that we work to a prescribed syllabus.

I am told that a few of the more serious students, bent upon making rapid progress, prefer the lecture to questioning and discussion, which they think involves waste of time. I have not changed my opinion on this account. We do not undertake to traverse the subject at the rate of the strongest members of the class; that would leave the weaker members hopelessly at fault. Moreover, even the stronger members of an elementary class profit more than they know by deliberate and even slow teaching. But there are limits which must not be passed. Sound practical judgment is wanted to prevent either haste or tiresome dawdling.

Every science has ways of its own, and I will not say that what I find to answer in biology would do equally well in chemistry or physics. But it seems to me probable that good will be done by making all elementary scientific lectures less descriptive and more disciplinary, by giving the class more to do and less to write down.

Since the last paragraph was printed in the *Journal of Education* my colleague, Prof. Smithells, has tried the livelier method in his chemical teaching. He furnishes me with the following account of his experience :—

"A few years ago the increasing number of students coming to the College with some previous training in Chemistry led me to establish a sort of higher junior class. This class, which includes also some second year students, numbers about thirty. The meetings of the class have been taking more and more the form of conferences, and we now very seldom have a lecture. I believe that the change has added very much to the efficiency of the teaching. In the first place, the students are led to depend mainly on themselves for getting mere information of the text-book kind, for I make no attempt to cover the whole ground of facts. In the second place, the conference brings to light many difficulties and misunderstandings which a teacher might never suspect to exist, but which, being laid bare, give a great opportunity for useful comment. In the third place, the teacher, freed from the burden of being text-book and expositor in one, is able to devote himself to giving students the right point of view in relation to facts they already know. This is a great thing in Chemistry, in which science an apparent want of logical continuity is so marked a feature. Chemical information is exceedingly apt to be miscellaneous and disconnected, and the teacher's hardest task is to teach the student to link one set of facts and phenomena to another. I believe that neither the tongues of men nor of angels will do this through formal lectures to junior students. Unfortunately, in my most elementary class, the numbers are so large and the individuals so varied in their capacity and in the time they are spending in the laboratory, that the conference system is impossible, and I have to do what I can by means of formal lectures. But I only regard these as giving a preliminary survey of the ground. In Biology, where all your students come untrained, and where they march in line so far as laboratory work is concerned, you have an enviable advantage.

"I should like to say that, in my opinion, formal lecturing to *schoolboys* on Chemical Science is a most mischievous practice. I have had a long and painful experience of the results."

So far I have been speaking of college lectures only. I am told that in schools the practice of lecturing is on the increase. This seems to me likely to be a change for the worse. The younger the pupil, the greater the need of a method which is searching and animated, which frequently changes the speaker, which takes note of the difficulties of individual boys and girls. I have found that the junior classes in college profit more by teaching than by lecturing, and I should be slow to believe that school classes profit more by lecturing than by teaching.

READING ALOUD IN THE FAMILY.

It is a pleasant practice to read aloud by turns some book entertaining to all. A quarter of an hour at breakfast and perhaps half an hour when the little ones are in bed may often be agreeably spent in this way.

The kind of conversation that goes on at table and round the fireside is one of the great means of developing the intelligence of children. To be brought up in a family where the talk is all about business and gossip and things out of the newspapers is nothing short of a calamity.

It is good that children should learn to love books. Not only should they know how to get information from books, but they should know how to get pleasure out of them. I would teach a child some respect even for the visible printed page. The good books of the household should be bound in a durable and attractive style. They should be carefully handled, not dog's-eared or thumb-marked or scorched by being held against the fire. When the young ones, grown up into men and women, think of the tea-table or fireside of the old home, let them associate with the bright hearth and the lamp and the hissing urn the reading that taught and amused them.

I will mention some of the favourite readings with my own youngsters. The things which succeeded best were those which pleased old and young alike. Books written for children did not turn out so well. I think the children would rather share the enjoyment of the grown-ups than have an entertainment all to themselves. Now for what I can remember as successful: Anson's Voyage; Scott's Journal of a Voyage to the Hebrides, in Lockhart's Life, and many other bits from the same life; Scott's Lady of the Lake and Marmion; parts of Macaulay's History, such as the Restoration of the Coinage, the Siege of Derry, and the Trial of the Seven Bishops; the Narrative of Linsenbarth, in Carlyle's Frederick the Great; the escape of Charles the Second after the Battle of Worcester, in Clarendon's History; scenes from Goldsmith's Good-Natured Man; Tour in the North of England, from Gray's Letters; Dickens's Christmas Chimes; Lamb's Essays of Elia; Chaucer's Nonne Preste's Tale, much shortened and slightly modernized; selections from Washington Irving's Sketch-book, Bracebridge Hall, etc.; M'Carthy's History of our own Times; parts of Gibbon's Autobiography; the Sir Roger de Coverley papers in the Spectator.

Every one took turns in reading. Pains were

taken about clear enunciation. No attempt was made to get up the passages read. If conversation arose naturally out of the reading, it was encouraged, but never pressed. An atlas was often sent for, to clear up points of geography. Signs of weariness among the younger members of the family were immediately attended to.

SCHOOL LESSONS IN DRAWING.

When a new student comes into our biological laboratory, we have generally to teach him to draw. It is a necessary part of his work to set down on paper the true shapes of a great number of natural objects, and this he has hardly ever learned to do beforehand. I think that not one student in twenty can make creditable representations of the objects put before him in his first week of laboratory work. A considerable proportion are disinclined to attempt any sort of drawing, though they do not grumble over it as they used to do. The ways of the laboratory are now known to students before they enter it, and they accept in silence a rule which takes no account of individual preferences or past training. After a term's work, nearly every student in a large class will be found to draw at least moderately well; after a year's work, nearly every student can draw well enough. By drawing well, I mean setting down accurately and neatly the shape of a complicated object.

Natural aptitude counts for something in this business, but not for so much as we might expect. Students who are distinguished for industry and intelligence are nearly always good at biological drawing. This is some indication that the work is essentially mechanical.

The drawing taught in most schools is of no use at all for our purpose. You may learn by copying from the flat certain tricks of what may be called *symbolic drawing*; for instance, how to produce rapidly a pattern which is by interpretation the foliage of a willow. You may get some notion of shading and of artistic management in the same way, but the biologist cares little about these things. We want no dexterous touches. A clean, firm stroke with a hard pencil is insisted upon. Shading is discouraged, and especially all kinds of laboured shading. Stippled shading, which costs an hour per square inch, is a mockery. If colour is required at all, it is diagrammatic colour, laid on as a flat wash.

I encourage my students to be as business-like as possible in their drawings. The maxim of some French schools is attended to:—*ébauchez toujours.* First sketch in the whole object, next put in the principal details, lastly the minor details. If there is much repetition of parts in the object, do not repeat them every time in the drawing. Draw one arm of the starfish carefully, and leave the others in the rough. Always think of the use to which the drawing is to be put, never of the credit which is to be got by it.

All persons who follow active occupations could profit by the kind of drawing which we practise in a biological laboratory. I suppose it would be called freehand drawing, because no instruments are required, but in every other sense it is mechanical drawing. This is the drawing which helps you to give orders to a carpenter, or to make scientific book-illustrations. It is the representation of definite fact with as little distortion, as little coloration by the imagination, as can possibly be contrived. Threads at measured intervals, ruled lines across the eyepiece of the microscope, and any other device which helps to get rid of exaggeration and to express realities, are appropriate to this method.

An art so useful in every-day operations has a strong claim to a place in the school-course. If I were a schoolmaster, I should teach it by means of map-drawing. Maps drawn strictly to scale, neatly coloured and lettered, teach a great part of geography admirably. The boys and girls who make them for themselves learn a good deal from them besides geography.

The simple and extremely useful art of tracing

should also be practised early. Mathematical instruments are excellent too, but it is not every boy who can be trusted with them. I have seen a schoolboy make a dart of a pair of dividers, and fashion a keel for his boat out of a brass protractor.

So far as we have gone, the art of drawing can be taught to everybody, whether possessed of artistic gifts or not. When quality of line begins to be considered, we pass out of purely mechanical drawing. Right emphasis by shading depends still more upon artistic feeling. If we aim at obtaining such a mastery of line and shadow as is requisite for the faithful representation of natural objects possessed of some degree of beauty, we must discourage the pen, on account of its inevitable bias, and use the brush freely. Line work of the best kind is not, I believe, attainable with the pen, and pencil has neither strength nor permanence.

Designing for work to be afterwards carried out is an excellent means of stimulating invention. It requires, of course, natural gifts which are far from universal. When the boy does fret-work, or wood-carving, and the girl embroidery, why should they not try to work to their own designs? Some will succeed, as I know by actual experience, and those who do will be very much the better for it. An experienced adviser is absolutely necessary to control the work, to point out where the design is over-ambitious or unsuited to the material, to correct bad management of repeats, and so on.

Now we have reached the threshold of fine art. Here I stop. Whether you can ever make an artist of a school-boy I don't know, but I think I should not try. The management of brush and pencil, together with the matter-of-fact representation of natural objects on paper, are of use to everybody, and everybody can learn them. I wish that the schools would teach so much, and leave fine art in all its forms to a later stage and other masters.

GEOGRAPHY AND MAP-DRAWING.

I entertained for many years a prejudice against Geography as a school subject. It seemed to me a mere collection of facts, wanting alike in organic coherence and in methods of its own. The only excuse for this serious mistake is furnished by some of the text-books of geography, which are encyclopædic, devoid of suggestion, and dominated by the idea that whatever is not taught in school is knowledge lost for ever. The writers of school manuals forget that the man of business has his atlas, his gazetteer, and often his encyclopædia. Where his recollection of lessons given long ago in school is faint, he can immediately supply himself with the information wanted. The schoolmaster will have done his part if his pupils have a good general notion of the world, a particular knowledge of certain parts of the world, and a fair stock of curiosity about unfamiliar countries.

I was, in the end, converted by my own boys, to whom I often address Wordsworth's lines:

> "Could I but teach the hundredth part
> Of what from you I learn!"

One and all they took to Geography like ducks to water. Map-drawing was their favourite in-door amusement. They learned from their own maps the shape and size of the chief countries, and the position of the great cities. It became a favourite game at meals to puzzle one another with hard geographical questions, such as: Name the chief American cities which begin with M; or, What places would be passed through by a straight line drawn from London to Moscow? The map led them on to elementary astronomy; it taught them to draw to scale, to lay on colours, to letter neatly, and in a certain degree to keep their fingers and papers clean. This last remark needs explanation. I don't mean to claim more than this, that the exigencies of map-drawing sent the boys many a time to wash their hands when public opinion was not operating. How often have I seen the wet afternoon beguiled with atlas and pen and paint-brush! Let me here record my gratitude!

Map-drawing, and the various inquiries which

sprang out of it, were one of the chief means by which these particular boys developed their own faculties. Not very much was done for them by parents or schoolmasters. They did it for themselves and for one another.

Geography and map-drawing were in this case associated with collecting and elementary astronomy. In the school it would be well to make the ties more strong. Latitude and longitude, globe-problems, the clock of the heavens, join on naturally to the map. So do geological sections and fossil-hunting, the mounting of dried plants, and botany. The link may be very slight, nothing common to the two studies except that large sheets of paper are required by both, but it is enough. How often does mere accident lead grown men to take up what may prove the master-pursuit of their lives.

ARITHMETICAL PRECISION.

An article in *Nature*, by Mr. Sydney Lupton,[1] first directed my attention to this subject, and led me to see that there is something in the school-teaching of arithmetic which needs reform. The only justification for returning to a subject which has already been clearly and impressively handled is that Mr. Lupton addressed his remarks to men

[1] *Nature*, Vol. XXXVII., January 5, 1888.

of science, and treated many sides of a large question. I propose to treat one side only, and to consider it in the elementary manner suitable to readers who are not specialists. This course is obviously the only one possible to a writer whose arithmetic is a mere tool for everyday use, and who can only attempt to apply what he has learnt from others.

By *precision* we may denote the degree of detail attempted in any statement. Precision may be real or imaginary, useful or useless. If I say that there are 123,441 inhabitants in a certain city, that piece of information is, in intention at least, very precise. It may be wrong, in which case the precision is perfectly useless. If true, it may be useful or not, according to circumstances. If you want to levy a head-tax, it may be important to know the exact number of heads. If you want to indicate the size of the city in comparison with others, or to determine the death rate, it will probably be best to drop the units, tens, and hundreds, and work from the nearest number of thousands.

For some purposes a high degree of precision in numerical statement is not only aimed at, but regularly achieved. What is more, it has a practical value. In the revenue returns the odd pounds are quoted, and, if we could get at the original statement, we should probably find shillings and pence as well. We are told that the Customs for 1891-92 amounted to £19,828,309. This statement is extremely precise, but it is also (if no mistake has been made in quoting) strictly accurate, and every figure is useful. Had the last figure been changed to 8 in the books of the Treasury, some one would have been called upon to account for the mistake, for it would have cost the State a pound sterling.

Even in money matters, however, we may easily use by inadvertence expressions which are uselessly precise. When you quote large sums, remember that interest will quickly affect the total, unless you are as careful about the date as about the amount. Our National Debt grows at the rate of about £40 a minute, so that, if you would have us know to a pound how great it is, you must tell us the day, hour, and minute for which the calculation is made.

The precision aimed at in a numerical statement is best measured by the number of significant figures. It makes no difference what is the place of the first figure. If the figures are the same, we may move the decimal point to right or left without affecting the precision of the statement: 21, 2·1, ·21 are equally precise. Suppose that in the second place 1 has been put for 0, the error is an error of 5 per cent., irrespective of the decimal point. In the same way, the precision of a map is estimated by the amount of detail given, not by the scale, though a large scale gives greater facilities for detail. An engraved map, a lantern slide reduced from it by photography, and an enlarged image cast upon a screen are (apart from distortion) equally precise, though very different in size.

An appearance of extraordinary precision is often obtained by mere manipulation of the figures. Suppose that you have determined, with as great exactness as your telescope and clock allow, the time occupied by the revolution about the sun of a particular planet. You can by mere arithmetic get from that measurement the angular space traversed by the planet in twenty-four hours, and you can, if you please, give your result to 100ths of a second. This result may greatly exceed the accuracy attainable by direct observation, and can hardly be useful unless a high multiple is taken, and the last places dropped, when it may come back into the region of practical use.

Whether the precision aimed at by astronomers is always useful, I do not venture to affirm or deny. In another branch of science, viz., chemical analysis, an appearance of extreme precision is sometimes got by mere arithmetic, and used for mere display. The third place of decimals, where the first was not to be relied upon, used to be common in results of analysis, but modern chemical opinion declares pretty strongly against such practices.

Mr. Lupton gives an amusing example of over-precision with its frequent attendant miscalculation:

On page 84 of the first edition (the second has been corrected) of Prof. Huxley's admirable Physiography, we read: "The weight of air on a square mile is about 590,129,971,200 lbs., and the carbonic acid which it contains weighs not less than 3,081,870,106 lbs., or about 1,375,834 tons. The weight of the carbon in the carbonic acid is 371,475 tons."

This short statement contains excellent examples of many of the common arithmetical slips and errors. The first number is ten times too great and not quite accurately calculated from the data

$$(5280)^2 \times 144 \times 14\cdot 73 = 59{,}133{,}431{,}808.$$

Multiplying this by $\frac{\cdot 05321}{100}$, the proportion by mass of carbonic acid in the air, we obtain 31,464,899; here, besides a slip, the number is again multiplied by ten. The pounds are reduced to tons correctly, but there is a slip in the reduction of carbon, since

$$\frac{1375834 \times 3}{11} = 375{,}227.$$

. . . .

Thus, Prof. Huxley gives the tenth figure, 6, in the expression for the amount of carbonic acid on a square mile, ignoring the facts that while the percentage of carbonic acid varies in the first figure, its density is not known to the fourth, and the pressure of the air varies in the second.

It is not uncommon for geologists to affect great

ARITHMETICAL PRECISION.

precision in calculations which rest upon the loosest data. The thickness of a formation is given to the odd yard, the rate of formation *guessed at*, and the result quoted to ever so many significant figures. One Alexander Crichton in 1825 ascertained that the London clay was formed 6829 years ago! In the first edition of the Origin of Species, Darwin estimates the time required for the erosion of the Weald at 306,662,400 years, but drops the whole thing in the later editions, having found it too risky. Sir A. Geikie gives the annual discharge of sediment from the Mississippi as 7,459,267,200 cubic feet. Is the first figure, or even the number of the figures, quite beyond doubt?

These over-precise estimates remind us of President Kruger's claim of £1,677,938 3s. 3d. for damage, "material, moral, and intellectual," caused by Jameson's Raid.

Precision beyond what the data justify and beyond the requirements of real business is always to be condemned. It is not workmanlike to throw away time and labour without increasing the value of the product. Unnecessary figures, even if accurate, are distracting, and there is a real risk of their leading to error. For instance, any one can see at a glance that $6000 \times 3 = 18,000$. But if for mere display you take, not round numbers, but numbers which affect a greater precision, such as $5943 \times 2{\cdot}9907$, you will be much more likely to get wrong, and the mistake is very apt to occur in the position of the decimal point, unless certain common-sense precautions are taken, which will presumably be unfamiliar to the over-precise computer. Thus, while you are straining to get exactness in figures which are of no consequence, you may get your result ten times too large or ten times too small.

When we deal with numbers which are so complex as to be unmanageable, we may make mistakes of any magnitude whatsoever. The greatest arithmetical mistake I have ever heard of arose by no great carelessness, and might be made by any one who was manipulating figures which had slipped out of his control. Some fifteen years ago two eminent physicists put forth a new theory of terrestrial magnetism, based on lengthy calculations. The theory was at length refuted by the discovery that in one place − had been put in place of +. This error, to the schoolboy's mind venial if not negligible, had the stupendous effect of dividing instead of multiplying by the square root of the number of centimetres in the earth's radius. The result was about 600,000,000 times too small.[1]

Over-precision is often connected with that tendency to put mechanical labour in the place of

---

[1] The history of this mistake may be traced in *Proc. Physical Soc.*, 1880.

thinking, which is so common among mankind. Looking the other day at a child's drawing of a dog, I found that the dog had only two legs, and no ears or tail. The little artist had made some progress with his outline when it suddenly occurred to him that a dog is hairy, and that hairs would be easy to draw. Accordingly he began to draw hairs, and went on till his time or his energy was used up. That is very like a good deal which goes by the name of science. I am sorry to say that natural history, the science with which I have most to do, is encumbered by multitudes of facts which are recorded only because they are easy to record.

A very precise arithmetical statement should be called upon to justify itself. We should ask whether the data are exact; whether two careful and experienced persons, starting from the things measured, weighed, or counted, would get the very figures quoted. We should then ask whether all these figures are necessary for some scientific or practical purpose.

The precision attainable and desirable differs greatly according to the department of work in which the question arises. In money-matters, as we have seen, a very unusual degree of precision is demanded, partly because of the facilities afforded by coinage, and partly because mankind cares a great deal about the result. If the units are pounds, both parties to the bargain will take great pains to get the right figure, even if there are several figures in front of it.

Time also can be very precisely measured, and hence arises an exactitude of quotation in excess of practical needs. Still we do attend to intervals of five minutes, that is, we divide the day into two hundred and eighty-eight parts for purposes of common business. Racing time-keepers note seconds, and fractions of seconds, but the whole time measured is very short. Astronomers subdivide very minutely in some cases, but many of their refinements are matters of arithmetic rather than of actual measurement. Dates are usually needlessly precise. The historian or biographer often gives the month and day of the month when the year would suffice for every purpose.

Of all measures [says Mr. Lupton], those of time are most frequently and most accurately made. Public clocks are far more numerous than public standards of length or mass, and in 1880 the value of the clocks and watches imported amounted to £880,000. Few persons carry a foot-rule, costing, say 1s., but many a watch costing more than £2. Even among engineers but little attention is paid to lengths less than $\frac{1}{64}$ of an inch; and few common balances indicate a difference of $\frac{1}{100}$ of the load. But, according to Mr. Rigg ("Cantor Lectures on Watchmaking," 1881), a watch that does not vary more than half a second per diem, or $\frac{1}{172800}$, is frequently met with, while an accuracy of two or three minutes a week, $\frac{3}{10000}$, is attained even by cheap articles. It is no uncommon occurrence to meet with a chronometer which does not vary one-fifth of a second in twenty-four hours, or by about $\frac{1}{432000}$ of the time measured out.[1]

Mr. Lupton gives much-needed explanations as to the precision attainable in scientific measurement:

Under suitable conditions, the observation of one quantity can be made with great exactness. It is possible that Sir George Airy estimated $\frac{1}{100}$ of a second in a day, or $\frac{1}{8640000}$; that a balance can be made to estimate $\frac{1}{1000000}$ of the load. . . . and that Sir J. Whitworth measured the $\frac{1}{1000000}$ of an inch. These cases, however, are exceptional, and give quite a wrong idea of the accuracy attainable in ordinary observations and experiments, when several operations, each liable to error, have to be performed, and various corrections introduced by calculation from extraneous data. The more closely we examine work of the highest accuracy, the more convinced we become of the truth of the statement of Thomson and Tait (page 333): "Few measurements of any kind are correct to more than *six* significant figures." . . . The great majority of experiments in physics, chemistry, biology, geodesy, mensuration, navigation, and crystallography, are not to be trusted beyond the fourth or fifth figure.

It is to be remarked that these are examples not of the ordinary, but of the extreme, precision possible in the several subjects. In many physical measurements, for instance, errors of 1 per cent. are considered harmless and inevitable.

[1] "Time," in *Nature*, February 14, 1889.

Now let us turn to methods, and see how we are to avoid the waste and distraction which come of over-precision. I dare say that not a few schoolmasters will defend their present methods, as one actually did, by saying: "I teach my boys to work accurately; they can simplify as much as they please when they come to actual business." I have seen over and over again that they do not, and cannot, simplify, unless they have been trained to do so. A grown man will multiply out by three or four significant figures, and *afterwards* reduce to round numbers. The habit of using concise methods must be learned, and it is hard to pick it up when youth is once past.

I would, on all grounds, urge that the schoolboy should be continually exercised with easy examples, the only ones which are frequent in practice. Instead of being set to work out lengthy results mechanically, let him ordinarily have easy sums which cannot be done without a little thought. Let the young computer be trained to consider the nature and conditions of every problem. What is the order of magnitude of the expected result? Will it be in tens, or hundreds, or what? Then get the leading figure or two by a rapid approximation. Consider how many significant places are really wanted. Get those, and then stop. It should be considered a fault to give distinctly superfluous figures. Warn the schoolboy of the danger of getting the important figures or even the decimal point wrong, while he is labouring to obtain useless accuracy in the last figures.

A very few schools teach the boys to begin to multiply by the figure of highest place value, and then by the lowest. A very few also practise contracted multiplication and division. These methods should be familiar to all boys who have begun to apply their arithmetic at all. The slide rule and four-figure logarithms should come in at the same stage, which in many schools is marked by the beginning of chemical calculation.

I must not get too detailed, lest it should be discovered how much I have myself to learn on these matters. There are many well-known and excellent school books which teach contracted methods and approximations.[1] What we now want is to have these things brought into the schoolroom for daily use.

Some day (though I fear that the day is still distant) boys and girls will learn, while still at school, to apply their arithmetic and geometry to real business—scientific, statistical, industrial, and commercial. Then the sums will grow shorter, the slide-rule and the table of logarithms will become familiar, contracted methods and approxi-

[1] Langley's little book on *Computation* (Longmans, Green & Co.) can be recommended.

mations will be explained and practised, Euclid will disappear for ever as a school book, solid geometry will come in earlier. I, for one, long to see that day: first, because it will be so profitable to learn betimes the actual methods of the work-a-day world, and, further, because the scholars will be relieved of much useless drudgery. They will, let us hope, be set to learn, not so much what is in the books, as what they have to use, that week or next. They will practise every process which saves time and labour, and will learn, by experience, what degree of precision is at once attainable and useful in a particular sort of work.

ELEMENTARY GEOMETRY.

When we think that a boy is old enough to study Geometry with advantage, we put Euclid's Elements before him, and bid him learn and say the propositions one after another. For some months at least, and in poor schools for the whole time, he learns Geometry in no other way. Is this a sound method of teaching?

Any teacher who has studied the principles of his art will reply, No. It cannot be right to set before a boy a worked-out system of any kind. The boy is to find out for himself, to answer questions which his teacher sets, and by and by to set and answer questions of his own. That a text-book, and one particular text-book too, is prescribed shows that our procedure is artificial. The natural course would be to put easy problems, and let the boy apply what small experience he has already gained to their solution.

The well-instructed teacher will require further that, whatever method is adopted, it shall satisfy these other fundamental conditions. The course must be graded in point of difficulty, easy things being taken first. One thing must be studied at a time, so that the boy shall not be distracted by needless change. Yet there must be variety, lest he tire of the monotony. He must learn by doing, and must be encouraged to apply every new bit of knowledge to practical problems. Euclid's Elements satisfy none of these conditions. The difficulties are not graded. Technical and abstruse definitions have to be mastered before anything is proved or done. Long, subtle, and highly artificial demonstrations appear as early as the fourth and fifth propositions of the first book. There is no intelligible sequence in the propositions, and the boy does not know where he is being led, nor why he glances from straight lines to triangles, and from triangles to parallel lines. But his love of variety is not always gratified; he is kept upon the subdivisions of rectangles until he is sick of them. Euclid's results are so remote from practice that for a good while the boy can do nothing with them. If he is fond of mechanical drawing, or making models of crystals, or surveying, Euclid will help him but little. The boy will turn to some book of Practical Geometry, which will show him how these things are done, probably with very little rational explanation. Euclid is for a good while, always for some boys, a thing out of relation to worldly affairs, a singular geometrical method, with difficulties and conditions of its own, which the school-boy finds unintelligible. If, for example, it is required to halve a straight line or an angle, common sense suggests various ways which Euclid totally rejects. They are not according to the rules of the game.

What the rules of the game really are, no beginner can fully understand. Euclid has set himself a serious and difficult task; he seeks to deduce from the smallest possible number of general principles, and by the fewest and simplest means the geometry known two thousand years ago. Discoveries of later date, such as those which involve the mensuration of the sphere, do not of course come in at all. Now, what can the school-boy make of such an enterprise as that which Euclid proposes? Untrained in abstract thought, he has to follow a long and slow process of demonstration, whose very postulates seem unnatural. By the time he has fully grasped Euclid's idea, he has already begun to abandon it in practice. Euclid will have no contact between Geometry and Arithmetic, but before the boy has quite worked through his Euclid he is introduced to far more powerful methods, which rely on the combination of Arithmetic and Algebra with Geometry. Euclid teaches him that it is not good form to draw conclusions from principles outside the very short list which has been adopted as self-evident. Experimental science restrains itself within no such limits, but uses all the certain knowledge which it can discover. To the school-boy this distinction, by which a method which is regarded as natural and indispensable in everything but Geometry is scouted in Geometry as illegitimate, is for a long time perfectly unintelligible, and I rather think that it is only the stronger minds that ever grasp its historical and logical meaning.

I take the very first opportunity of pointing out that the better teachers, even in English schools, do not trust wholly to Euclid. When some progress has been made they set problems and deductions, based upon propositions which are by this time familiar, and the teaching at once begins to take a more interesting form. Important truths and methods are introduced, which are not to be found in Euclid. The boy works for himself, and learns by doing. Many men who have been put through such a course of Euclid riders will tell you that it brightened their intelligence more than anything else that they did at school.

This will seem to be a considerable admission. If Euclid with riders has such merit, why should we not keep our Euclid after all? To this I would answer that the merit lies partly in the Geometry and partly in the efforts of the boys to attain new results by their own exertions. I will not praise Euclid for it until I am satisfied that this method, which I believe to be the true one, can be more successfully worked with Euclid than with any other text-book of Geometry. It is because I would have it practised earlier and more widely that I would banish Euclid from at least the junior forms of every school.

All who have read Plato's "Meno" will recollect the pleasant little lesson in Geometry which is to be found there. Socrates maintains that all our knowledge is recollection, and that the teacher merely makes evident to us what we unconsciously knew beforehand. Since Meno finds this a hard saying, Socrates calls for a boy, and Meno's slave, who has never been taught by anybody, is sent for. Socrates, by drawing figures and putting questions, draws from the boy the measure of a square in terms of its sides, and makes him prove that the area of the square is half that of the square upon its diagonal. We may, perhaps, demur to the conclusion which Socrates triumphantly claims, viz., that the boy knew these things before, though no one had taught him. The lesson is chiefly valuable to us as an example of the way to give geometrical notions to an untrained mind. The boy is made to recognize by the eye the equality of certain parts of the figure drawn for him. He may repeat the construction on any scale, and use any instruments he pleases for the sake of greater accuracy, but the result will be the same. That is enough at the time; the notion of strict logical proof deduced from the smallest possible number of assumptions, and these as nearly self-evident as can be contrived, properly belongs to a later stage of mental development, and a mind unpractised in Geometry neither requires conditions so rigid, nor profits by their observance.

Truth may be arrived at by two ways: (1) by observing and trying, which we call induction; or (2) by reasoning from known principles, which we call deduction. Both are valuable, but induction is the more indispensable of the two. Induction must precede deduction, for (to decide summarily a point which has been hotly contested) the very principles with which deduction starts have to be drawn by induction from experience. In that concrete and ill-mastered science which constitutes the vast bulk of our knowledge of matters of fact, we attain nearly all our results by induction, and use deduction chiefly for verification and exposition. The child reasons inductively, and cannot pursue the other method without careful direction. It would seem to follow that the abstract truths of Geometry must be first appreciated by observation, then confirmed by daily use, and only in a later stage deduced by strict reasoning from a few comprehensive principles.

If we adopt this method all the work will be congenial and intelligible. We shall not force the unwilling child to pursue a train of thought which he could by no means have devised, and in which he can only be passively carried along. We shall encourage him to do things for which he is really fit, to solve problems which he will be able immediately to apply. We shall teach a Geometry which will be of use in the manufacture of models and Christmas cards and boxes; it will have points of contact with all that he sees and all that he does. Deductive Geometry has its place too, but for this the time has not yet come.

It will naturally happen that the first exercises in Geometry will be problems rather than theorems, things to be done rather than things to be proved. The problem is the more interesting to the untrained mind, and its successful accomplishment a more obvious gain. It is probable that geometrical discovery has largely arisen out of problems suggested by practical needs, and solved by an ever-growing theory. To the beginner there will of course be no such thing as absolute proof; we shall show that every triangle we have drawn or cut out has its angles equal to two right angles; we shall not show that the same thing is true of every imaginable triangle. The distinction need not be insisted upon with a junior class, which is not at all interested in abstract discussions upon the nature of proof; it will be thoroughly in place when Deductive Geometry is taken up.

I should begin by carrying a little further the Geometry of the Kindergarten. Show how to make a variety of figures by paper-folding. Classify quadrilaterals and triangles. Give out exercises which require circles and arcs made with compasses. Show by folding that a paper triangle has three angles which are equal to two right angles, and that its area is half the rectangle contained by its base and its height. Teach the use of the divided scale, the diagonal scale, and the protractor. Measure the areas of a variety of surfaces. Show the use of dissection and transposition in proving the equality of certain areas. Show how to build up a variety of regular solids out of cards. Make an instrument which will read angles with tolerable accuracy, and employ it to take heights, and lay down the true shape of a field.

Of course the teacher new to the work will gladly profit by the experience of those who have gone before him. The following books, all of which contain useful exercises, are recommended by Mr. E. M. Langley in a letter to *Nature*: (1) W. G. Spencer's "Inventional Geometry" (Williams & Norgate). An excellent general guide, which may be corrected and extended according to the views of each teacher. (2) Paul Bert's "Experimental Geometry" (Cassell & Co.). (3) H. Perigal's "Geometric Dissections and Transpositions" (Assoc. Impr. Geom. Teaching). (4) A. J. Pressland's "Geometrical Drawing" (Rivington, Percival & Co.). More rational than many other text-books, which are satisfied with getting their figures, and care little about geometrical knowledge. (5) T. Sundara Row's "Geometrical Exercises in Paper-Folding" (Addison & Co., Madras). Many more elementary exercises would be useful. The author advances rather rapidly to the higher parts of the subject. (6) A. Pickel's "Geometrie der Volksschule" (Bleyl und Kämmerer, Dresden).

From these books any competent teacher of Geometry can easily construct his own course. No book at all need be put before the class. Experimental Geometry, thus taught, may very well occupy two or three years. It should leave the pupil familiar with geometrical terms, tolerably expert in the mensuration of plane and solid figures, and well practised in easy problems.

Let us suppose our school-boy to have got so far as this, and to have reached an age (fourteen or fifteen) when some power of abstract reasoning may be looked for, if his teaching has been rational. We can now, if we please, teach him Deductive Geometry.[1] What can we hope to do for him thereby? Deductive Geometry will teach him what strict proof means. It will teach him to follow out the consequences of an admitted statement. It will give him examples, the most complete that can be found, of constructive reasoning, which builds up an elaborate structure of unquestionable solidity upon a few simple and self-evident propositions. Deductive Geometry should also help him to throw his geometrical notions into the form of extremely general statements, which can be easily remembered and easily applied. The course of Deductive Geometry, dealing largely with properties which have already become familiar, should be rapid, its language clear and terse. Its method should be intelligible, its classification simple, in order that the train of reasoning should be

[1] The Deductive Geometry should not come in suddenly. While the pupil is working through his course of Practical Geometry, he may be exercised in easy deductions, which gradually become more rigorous and more general.

recalled as easily as possible. How far does Euclid meet these requirements?

Euclid is open to some objections on the ground of strictness of proof, but the wonder is, considering the difficulty of his self-imposed task, that he comes off as well as he does. De Morgan has collected all the tacit assumptions which he could discover in Euclid's first six books in the Companion to the Almanack for 1849. Few of them are of great consequence, though it is a reproach to the editors of Euclid that they so often remain uncorrected in the new editions. Euclid has been often praised for the fewness and self-evident character of his first principles, but it would be hard to say why he does not greatly extend his postulates of construction. It is no offence against strict logic to assume that the middle point of a line or the middle line of an angle can be found, nor that two circles can be drawn with the same radius, nor that a perpendicular can be drawn to any straight line, or a tangent to any circle. Such possibilities of construction would render the course vastly more rapid and connected, while they would take nothing from the cogency of the proof. Euclid's method is extremely slow, and it costs much labour to establish certain general results which are of practical importance. When we come to apply our Geometry to Physics we are often driven to extend without proof the partial truths which have been arrived at in Euclid. Thus we continually want to use the proposition that all surfaces of similar figures, whether plane or solid, increase as the square of any linear dimension.[1] Euclid attains no such result, though he proves it in separate places for plane triangles and for plane polygons. Euclid's doctrine of proportion is so intolerable that it is omitted in actual teaching, only to be assumed, without pretence of geometrical proof, in the sixth book.

Euclid's artificial restrictions lead, as has been pointed out, to a most ingenious but eminently perplexing sequence of propositions; they render progress slow, and entail the proof of many things which have little or no permanent value. Out of some 180 propositions in the first six books I count about twenty-six[2] as necessary to be known,

---

[1] It is easy to prove that squares, and therefore all figures which are made up of squares, vary according to this law. But all surfaces can be resolved into infinitely small squares. Therefore the property holds good of all surfaces. In the same way all cubes, and therefore all solids, vary as the cube of any linear dimension. Imagine the horror of the Euclidean at having such a proof offered to him! Yet everywhere, outside of Euclid's Elements, he accepts and acts upon precisely similar proofs.

[2] Bk. I. 4, 5, 6, 8, 16, 26, 32, and its corollaries, 47; Bk. II. 12, 13; Bk. III. 18, 20, 21, 22, 31, 32, 35, 36; Bk. IV. 4, 5; Bk. VI. 1, 2, 3, 19, 20, 33.

though many of these require to be combined into more general propositions. The rest are only important as steps to other results. Euclid's phraseology is pedantic and cumbrous, and he takes up so much time in proving so little that a sound elementary knowledge of Plane and Solid Geometry, besides Trigonometry, might be easily got while a boy of equal ability was mastering Euclid alone. It is for these reasons that Euclid has been universally discarded in continental schools. The English-speaking nations have him all to themselves.

The advocates of improved teaching of Geometry are often met by an argument which I can only describe as amazing. How, it is asked, can we possibly examine if some of the candidates have learned their Geometry out of Euclid, and some out of another book? What a measure does this question afford of the domination of the examiner! First the examiner, then the teacher; perhaps the scholar may be allowed to come in third. All the candidates must be taught out of one book, for fear that the examiners may otherwise be unable to tell who is competent in Geometry and who is not! The argument is absolutely insular; cross the Channel, and you hear no more of it.

I wish all success to the Association for the Improvement of Geometrical Teaching. Improvement seems to be wanted rather badly.

CLASSICAL GRAMMAR AND LITERATURE.

[I wrote and published this paper with some misgivings, feeling that the subject could ill be passed over, but doubting my competence to handle it. It is with much satisfaction that I now find my opinions confirmed by far better judges. Mr. T. H. Matthews, headmaster of Bolton-le-Moors Grammar School, writing to the *Journal of Education* of November, 1896, supports my chief points. He is convinced that the classics will be swept out of the ordinary curriculum unless the exorbitant claims of the grammarians can be reduced. We must drop large slices of the grammar, and teach the thought. The natural tendency of all examinations for juniors is to concentrate attention upon what is capable of the most exact expression. Of all sides of language teaching, the grammatical is the most definite, the most exact, but by far the least formative. French should be learned before Latin. He would have no set books, and would have the grammar confined to questions arising out of the passages selected for translation. A little later appeared the New Supplement to the *Guide to the Choice of Classical Books*. The author, Prof. Joseph B. Mayor, points out in his preface the ordinary defects of the classical school. He thinks that too much is made of prose composition, and that too much stress is laid upon minutiæ. "It can never be too strongly insisted upon that the end of classical education, and its sole justification, is not to turn out philologers, but to train men." He feels it "disappointing and humiliating, that in so many cases the prolonged study of Latin and Greek seems to leave so very little trace behind." He would have the teacher "keep alive in his pupils the sense of the unity which connects together the parts of a great poem or other work of art." He too discourages examination by set books, and would substitute translation of unseen passages. Such sayings as these restore my peace of mind. I have not, I now feel persuaded, done an injury to enlightened teachers by my ignorant comments.]

We make considerable sacrifices for the sake of Latin and Greek, but I sadly fear that these sacrifices are seldom justified by the event. My own observation has taught me that only a small fraction of the boys who go through a classical school get any effective command of either language. I remember seeing a Christmas card, which had two lines of Pindar on it, handed round a company which contained several men more or less scholarly by profession, clergymen and schoolmasters. Remarks were made on a peculiarity in the Greek characters, but no one took any notice of the request of the ladies to have the passage translated. I have more than once seen how a few lines of Latin will bother, say a zoologist, who was at grammar school and University, but never read for classical honours. In fact, I think I am not putting the case too strongly in saying that you will hardly get a page of Latin or easy Greek read at sight, except by a man who has taken classical honours, or has followed classical studies for several years after leaving college.

My own classical attainments are so insignificant that I shrink from the appearance of showing the classical master how to teach classics. But it is not a matter for classical men alone. I have been a schoolboy; I have been a father of schoolboys; and I have seen things which not every classical master cares to study. It is worth while now and then to have a subject of education looked at from the point of view of men who have drifted into widely different pursuits, and who come in mature life to review the methods practised upon them in their boyhood. The great demands of time made by the classical master require to be justified by results of real importance. And it is not only classical men who have a right to be on the jury. Every grammar-school master, every parent of a grammar-school boy, is interested in the question whether Latin and Greek may fairly claim a third or even half of the school-time of every boy in such a school.

Latin, as all who know anything of it will admit, is very hard. The inflexions are numerous and bothering. But it is the construction of the sentence which is the real *crux*. Even a good Latinist, who can write a correct and easy Latin prose, will sometimes puzzle over a sentence of Livy in which every single word is perfectly familiar. All the modern languages of which I have the slightest knowledge can be mastered by any person of sound mind, provided that time and opportunity are given. But Latin requires certain gifts, and especially a power of appreciating subtle distinctions, which is by no means universal. Literary Latin has probably always required some special aptitude in the pupil. When Latin was the familiar language of the professional classes throughout Europe it was not that literary or classical Latin which we strive to teach in our schools. Even at Rome, in the days of Cicero, I doubt (how little right have I either to doubt or affirm!) whether the legionary and the shopkeeper had much effective command of Latin as written by a rhetorician. Cicero must have often spoken Greek to the Quirites, as to honest Casca in Shakespeare.[1]

The difficulty of Latin seems to justify cer-

---

[1] For more about this, the reader may be referred to "Le Latin Vulgaire," by Paul Monceaux, *Revue des deux Mondes*, July, 1891.

tain stipulations of the classical masters which are generally considered a little unreasonable. What can he do with only an hour a day during five or six years? The men who enjoy an easy command of Latin have been soaked in Latin, have at some time read Latin in quantity, to the almost complete exclusion of non-literary studies.

Latin is a very different language from French and German. You can begin these by reading and hearing, taking up such grammar as is indispensable, bit by bit. I remember how I began German. I wanted to read Baer's "Entwicklungsgeschichte," and I started with no help but a German dictionary. When I was through that one book, I had done enough to make German anatomy and zoology accessible to me. But set a man, new to Latin, down to Cæsar's "Commentaries," with nothing but a dictionary, and, if he makes out the meaning at all, it will be by guessing. After weeks of such work he will have made little solid progress. The Latin grammar cannot be taken for granted. The first interesting author you attempt to read requires abundance of it. Sooner or later, a great deal of Latin grammar has to be learnt—unless, indeed, you prefer to make it for yourself, as Scaliger gave out that he had done with the Greek grammar.

If the classical master were to claim four or

five years and two hours a day, I don't think he would ask too much, if at the end of the time a youth of fair abilities is to be able to use Latin for literary purposes. Verse-making and all accomplishments not necessary for intelligent appreciation of classical authors I do not include. Many schoolboys cannot spare so much time as this for Latin; others have neither inclination nor aptitude for it; others are ill-taught. The consequence is, that out of the army of young imps who set out with *musa, musae*, only a small fraction emerges at the other end of the business, able to take down their Tacitus and Cicero and read with understanding and moderate ease. The more advanced can, in after-life, at least make out Latin authors with the help of a dictionary; the less advanced half (or more than half?) know nothing which signifies. The grammar-school boy spends a large fraction of his time in mastering the grammar of a language which he is never destined to use. Tacitus and Cicero require preliminary studies so elaborate that, after spending years over them, he never reaches his Tacitus and Cicero at all. He lays a costly foundation for a structure which is never to be built. Surely there is some miscalculation in this! Surely it must be wrong for so many to undertake a task which so few accomplish!

The grammar-school boy need not be pitied if he has got some appreciation of the great ancient literatures. A man who is far short of being a great classic may still read the Latin or Greek authors with pleasure and profit. I know just such a case—a clergyman who took low honours at Oxford, and for nearly sixty years afterwards delighted himself and a circle of like-minded friends with the study of Horace. But what if there has been no love of literature in the case? What if the boy has read no authors with understanding? What if he brings away from school nothing more precious than an imperfect recollection of the Latin grammar? Heine expresses the bitter feeling of a man who has been forced to spend much of his youth upon studies which have borne no fruit. "As for Latin, madam, you can have no idea how complicated it is. The Romans would never have had time to conquer the world if they had not learnt the Latin grammar in their cradles. As to the nouns of the third declension—which make their accusative singular in *im*, and which in *em*—I paid careful attention to them betimes, so as to have them ready if I should want them in a hurry, and in many a sorrowful hour of after-life this has given me much inward calm and consolation."

What, then, are we to try? I would answer, take first the things which every boy can do, and afterwards the things which only the few can do. For example, let every boy in a grammar school learn French from nine to fourteen; let picked boys learn Latin from twelve onwards. It will offend some teachers to make French the introduction to Latin, instead of Latin the introduction to French. I would ask such to consider whether the French or Italian boy is at any disadvantage in learning Latin; whether he is not really at an advantage as compared with the English or German boy. French is easy; there is less grammar to get up, and what there is is not nearly so indispensable as in Latin. French can be taught orally; Latin is a dead language, and most of the literary Latin taught in schools was never in the full sense of the word living. Probably it always had to be learnt at school. The well-taught boy of fourteen should read French with ease, and use it to gratify such love of literature as he may chance to possess. No ordinary boy of fourteen can get any literature out of Latin. He is too much harassed with syntax and inflexions; he reads only so many lines a day. Fancy the effect of reading Macaulay's History at the rate of half a page a day! French authors have far easier access to the boy's mind; the persons, the situations, the thoughts are modern. Hence the schoolboy can see the fun of "Tartarin sur les Alpes"; he cannot see the fun of the "Iter Brundusii." French is the manageable thing, not too hard, not too remote; let every grammar-school boy get that. Latin is hard and remote; let those get it whose opportunities and inclinations favour the attempt.

Are the schoolboys who do not learn Latin and Greek to go without literature? Heaven forbid! Great as are the merits of the ancient classics, there is high literature outside them. The love of literature has burned bright in many a man who could read neither Latin nor Greek. I could wish that <u>literature and not grammar</u> should decide what classical authors should chiefly be read in schools. I am told that the copious reading of Homer is now somewhat discouraged. Homer does not furnish sufficient materials for the cultivation of a good Greek prose. But is there any Greek author who will do more to enliven the literary sympathies of the boy? Is there any Greek author more accessible to the busy professional man, who has forgotten much of his grammar, and hates to look up words in a dictionary? When the physician or lawyer craves a little of the refreshing influence of literature for that last hour of the day, when the house is quiet, and the cares of business lose their importunity, surely Homer has a charm beyond that of most other authors, living or dead. How that magnificent gallery of portraits, so human and so lively, touches the imagination! Or that panorama of scenes in the story of the wandering Ulysses—some grotesque, some simply natural, some pathetic, some stirring—is it not a rich possession to boy or man? Your high honour-man may perhaps, in after-life, read Demosthenes or Sophocles for pleasure. But for one that can enjoy these there are twenty who can enjoy Homer.

Do not say that the English translation can take the place of the old text. The music and the charm are not there. The lover of Homer who finds his Greek unsound in places will not despise a good English version. But there is no substitute for the Greek. We cannot forego, without real loss, the melodious passages which at length sink into the memory, and soothe many a tiresome journey or restless night. How much more melodious they would be if we had not imposed upon them our own barbarian pronunciation!

I could plead not less earnestly that the schoolboy in whom the love of literature has taken root may be taught to know Horace and Juvenal familiarly. Though I have forgotten nearly all the rules of Latin prosody, though I could not write a Latin prose without comic effects, I still, in my own blundering way, enjoy Horace and

Juvenal. What is the technical business of the grammarian to a man who spends the best of his time in the technical business of natural history? I would not undertake to carry along with me the rules and distinctions of the grammarian, even if I could learn them at a wish. They belong to another calling, and I do not covet them. But the *mitis sapientia* of Horace and the stern moral force of Juvenal I should be sorry to exchange even for greater command of the tools of my own calling.

The grammar-school master, the University tutor, or the public examiner who puts grammar in the first place and literature in the second hastens on the day when classical learning will be unjustly despised. The love of literature will incite men to make sacrifices. For among the few intrinsically good things possessed by man are noble literature, great pictures, and other high works of art. But when it comes to grammar and the rules of Greek prose, what are they that we should bow down and serve them? As means to an end, as helps to the understanding of an author, they have their place. But when the author is sacrificed to the grammar, when Homer must not be read copiously for fear of his effect upon Greek prose, grammar and composition are claiming too much. If technical business is to come first, why should we not go for the technical business of our own callings, and throw over Latin and Greek altogether?

A claim is sometimes put forward in favour of the Latin grammar as a faculty-training subject. I have no doubt that an enlightened teacher can get excellent drill out of it, but so he can out of other grammars and other subjects. To the small boy who is set to learn his Latin grammar by rote, it yields no more profit than it does pleasure. It is grammar as a consistent theory of language which is valuable as discipline, and, if there is one proposition concerning teaching as a means of discipline which is now to be taken as tolerably settled by the unanimity of the best judges, it is this, that theory must follow the acquisition of the concrete facts—first natural knowledge, then science; first languages, then grammar. If the Latin grammar with all its intricacies is saved for the few boys who can profit by it, and deferred even in their case to as late a stage of their studies as the practical exigencies of reading will admit, the better will be its effect as discipline.

The schoolmaster or professor, if he is zealous and fit, likes to have everything done well that is done at all. This love of technical excellence he shares with nearly all men whose heart is in their work. The professor of biology likes to see a clean dissection and a workmanlike drawing. The classical master must have the rules of grammar minded. Of what use is fine talk about literature and ethics, or the action of the soil and climate upon Greek poetry, or other high matters of that sort, if you cannot give the right accusative to a noun, or use the subjunctive in the right place? I have much sympathy with the classical master, and have noticed this abhorrence of slovenly grammar in all the best of the race whom I have chanced to know. Let us continue to teach the grammar as thoroughly as we know how, but to illustrate and form our rules, as much as possible, by the examples which come up in our authors. Grammar enforced by *live* examples is stimulating and not deadening. Such grammar does not hinder, but helps, the mastery of an author.

If such an ignoramus as I must confess myself to be may offer opinions on practical questions, I should like to say a word or two about first lessons in Latin. It seems to me lamentable that the excellent introduction known to past generations as "Henry's First Latin Book" should be allowed to drop out of use. It fulfilled a number of the conditions of a really good first book, and especially this, that every little bit of vocabulary or grammar was used as soon as learnt. There was no long course of learning by rote things whose use lay months in advance. The modern substitute, which continues to bear the old name, is quite a different book, in which a multitude of things which Arnold had made a point of leaving out as not of immediate application are diligently brought back again. Now the boy is taught a vast number of things which he will either carry or drop, but which he certainly will not use in this stage of his learning.

Is it not true that some of the methods of the classical master are too mechanical; that he relies a good deal, for example, upon written exercises corrected next day or the day after? Is it not true that he trusts too much to writing, and uses too little the sound of the spoken words? What I have indirectly got to know about the teaching of languages would lead me to expect good results from extempore exercises, given out *viva voce* in class, and corrected on the spot. Has not the teaching of Latin and Greek been hindered by the entire abandonment of colloquial speech in those languages? Roger Ascham and Sir John Cheke must needs break with the Latin of the monks, and it was they who set up that insular pronunciation which we are ashamed to produce before foreigners. Should we bless their memory for this, or should we attribute to their purism some part of the difficulty with which we arrive at even a moderate command of the ancient tongues?[1]

I have my doubts on these points. If I were a classical man, very likely I should have none. But if a sound classic were by chance to share such doubts, and to try whether the methods which win success in the teaching of French and German may not be in some degree applicable to Latin and Greek, he would render a service to education by telling his experience.

If Latin and Greek are to be taught, shall we get the most valuable results by subordinating the literature to the grammar, or by subordinating the grammar to the literature? The answer to this question will help to form our opinion on

[1] "Goulburn and I," says Dean Stanley, "endeavoured to wile away the time by sharpening our modern Greek upon the anvil of a Transylvanian boy. From modern we passed to ancient Greek, and from that to Latin, and in Latin the boy fairly put us to shame, not only from the fluency which his use of his own pronunciation gave him, but from the really idiomatic and almost classical way in which he expressed himself; and he was so proud of his victory that he laughed to scorn the very notion of our being teachers in the 'University of Oxford.' 'You teachers! when you can't talk it yourselves! In some obscure school, I suppose? Well, at any rate, you can only teach little boys!'; and at last ended by saying, with a look of the most supreme contempt: 'Discamus melius et tunc loquamur.'" ("Life of Stanley," Vol. I., page 268.)

other questions. If it appears that we must bring up the classical schoolboy mainly as a grammarian, and that the best test of his teaching is his Latin and Greek prose, I for one go over at once to Bain's curriculum. Give us science, history, literature (other than classical), grammar and composition (English and foreign), besides certain indispensable practical arts, and we shall do well enough. "The subtle incommunicable aroma of classical poetry is one of the luxuries of scholarship. The mass of students cannot reach it, and it may be bought too dear" (Bain).

Reformers of the grammar-school curriculum will have done a great service when they have carried these three points:—(i.) That the living foreign language shall come first, and then the dead language; (ii.) that the many shall learn the living language, and the few the dead language; (iii.) that the dead languages, when taught, shall be taught on human principles. Taught mechanically, they are not good things at all, but bad.

SCHOOL MUSEUMS.

I have had charge of museums in some form or other for thirty years, and have thereby learned as much about them as I am capable of learning. It was long my ambition some day to arrange a museum which should be really fit for the instruction of the people, and I have often thought what I would do when the time came. But the time has never effectively come; I have never had space and free play. I do not think that great sums of money are wanted, but space (not necessarily great space) and full liberty to select and arrange are indispensable.

A school museum should be arranged on the same lines as any other museum which is intended for the instruction of people who are not experts. What museums for experts should be I do not propose to consider. I will merely say in passing that they are far more important to the national welfare than is generally allowed, and that our notions as to adequate provision for them are at present distinctly narrow. The museum for experts will, of course, be arranged to meet the wants of experts, and will inevitably be to that extent dull and unintelligible to the majority of the people.

The school museum or popular museum will go wrong if it is worked on the lines of the museum for experts. The expert demands the maximum of completeness and method; you cannot refine too much for him, if your method is good. But the non-expert public, whether junior or senior, needs to be impressed and interested. The great risk is that of distraction. The collections intended to instruct the non-expert must not aim at completeness, lest they oppress his intelligence; they must tell him a little at a time, with every advantage of arrangement and grouping; they need not be either extensive or systematic. Long series of specimens—*e.g.*, of butterflies, birds' eggs, or minerals—should go into cabinets, where they will be sheltered from dust and sunlight, and cease to bewilder the young naturalist by their number and variety. We ought to provide opportunities for the collecting, sorting, and naming instincts, but not at the expense of our displayed collection, which should be luminous and telling, like a good book or a good picture.

Do not, if you can help it, make *selfish* collectors of your boys. Collecting may only gratify a sordid craving; it is sometimes an amiable weakness; now and then, it is carried on for the sake of the general good. Eagerness to possess must not be allowed to overpower the love of knowledge. To collect for the school museum may be honourable, while to collect for the gratification of a selfish instinct may be frivolous or even base. Warn the schoolboy that the passion for possessing rarities may make him an Apollyon or destroyer. I know of more than one botanical club, which visits every station of rare species within reach, and eradicates the plants without mercy for distribution as dried specimens. There are so-called naturalists who allow no kingfisher to live within many miles of them; others who seek out and impale every moth or butterfly which has an exchange value. When the collector points with pride to a long series of Purple Emperors or Large Blues, I try to let him know that I look upon him as an enemy to Natural History. Trading in species, either by purchase or exchange, should be steadily discouraged. It does no real good to science, no good to those who engage in it. Let the selfish collector exercise his ignoble instinct upon postage stamps.

The objects offered to the consideration of young and untrained persons should be selected with the greatest care. They should, of course, be grouped, but not in a mechanical way. Each group should form naturally around a particularly striking and interesting object, or else illustrate one definite and rather limited subject. Let us take a few examples.

It is important to bring home to young minds the former existence of animals and plants very different from any that now inhabit the earth. Local opportunities will naturally decide the choice of extinct forms. Any of the following will do very well if good of its kind: an ammonite, a belemnite, a trilobite, an ichthyosaur. Round your big and striking fossil you will group others, less complete, perhaps, but bringing out special points of structure. Then you will collect and arrange allied organisms of recent date, besides restorations, either in the form of drawings or models. But here be careful not to indulge your imagination without full knowledge, lest you produce monsters like those which Waterhouse Hawkins set up in the Crystal Palace grounds. Then you must contrive to suggest the great lapse of time since your fossil animal disappeared from the earth. You can do something by discovering steps or historical landmarks. Somewhere in the neighbourhood there is, we will suppose, an eleventh-century church, or the porch of one, standing on an alluvial river-flat. Raised river-gravels, pointing to a very different level for the river, contain, it may be, rude stone implements and mammoth bones. All these you will bring in by actual specimens, photographs, and coloured sections. Both sets of river-deposits lie upon the wasted surface of the chalk. This takes us back to the time when the chalk was worn into hill and valley, and to the still more remote time when the chalk was formed. A few explanations concerning chalk and Atlantic ooze will convey some vague sense of the slow accumulation of the chalk. So we go on till we have displayed all the tokens of successive ages and successive occupants of the surface of the earth which we require or can discover. Be slow to bring in numbers. The average rate of deposit of Atlantic ooze—so much in a century—and the like suppositions are very untrustworthy. Use printed cards in perfectly legible type for your explanations. It is often well to point out accessible books which give fuller information, but no really necessary explanation should be left to chance. It is well to banish written labels of every kind. Coal and some common coal-plants should also come in. They are easily procured and can be made to tell some part of their story without too great difficulty.

Many aspects of bird-life can be dealt with effectively. The structure of a bird in relation to its external conditions; the wing, feather, beak, and claw; the various forms and uses of these; nests and eggs—are a few among many points of interest. Or we may take the life histories of insects—the cabbage-white and its ichneumon, the vapourer, the silk-worm, and so on. We want all the stages of the insect, its food-plant, its constructions, its enemies, illustrations of its uses or its ravages, and so on. Boxes of pasteboard with glass fronts, about twelve inches by seven inches, are convenient for exhibition. The Natural History Museum at South Kensington shows what can be done to make birds and insects interesting to the public when the highest skill can be commanded.

I would also have living things in the school or

people's museum—tadpoles, soles and flounders, crayfish or lobster, developing trout, caddis-worms, dragon-fly larvae, utricularia, the sun-dew, and many more. Only those should be shown which thrive in confinement.

It is needless to say that remains of mediæval, Roman, and prehistoric times will be a great help, but in most cases they will be hard to procure. Certain industries may be effectively illustrated. Suppose that we select the production of a book. We want type, a composing-stick, stereotype, wood-blocks, a lithographic stone, bookbinders' tools, and examples of a book in all its stages from the unfolded sheet to the finished volume. Do not undertake many industries, and do thoroughly what you attempt. The good popular museum will everywhere show thought presiding over both mechanical labour and material objects; the bad museum will show mechanical labour getting to the top place, or else thought striving in vain to cope with a multitude of objects.

As to buildings and fittings, I can offer no useful general remark, unless it is this, that small and inexpensive rooms may be turned to good account. What is really essential and not easy to find is the right man—a man able to organize and to carry out, a man both enthusiastic and methodical, with power to interest many people and set them to work in a really profitable way. The rarity of such men is the one great difficulty in the way of a good school or popular museum.

EXAMINERS AND CANDIDATES.

I have never joined in the wholesale denunciation of public examinations, because I remember the days when public examinations were few, and exerted little influence upon the schools. How formal and unreal were the so-called school-examinations of forty or fifty years ago! I have belonged to a class who got up a single proposition of Euclid, and repeated it one after another to the examiner, who listened silently, and perhaps took it as proof of progress in geometry. The Oxford and Cambridge Locals, though they have now, particularly in the special subjects, become rather a hindrance than a help to the best teaching, were in their early days a great step forward. We shall always require the stimulus of the independent examination. Would that the examiners were more enlightened than they commonly are in 1897!

Examination of persons unknown is very difficult. It is easy to examine your own classes, but to examine a crowd of persons whom you have never seen, by printed papers only, is anxious work. The examiner who strives to be useful and not mischievous must continually say to himself that he is there to discover knowledge and capacity, not to discover ignorance. It is easy to take this attitude for the first quarter of an hour, but the attention flags, and before long an effort is necessary if we are not to subside into some stupid mechanical routine, such as marking by the mistakes.

Setting the questions is the most cheerful part of the business. It gives one an opportunity of bringing out one's pet views, and of favouring or discouraging particular ways of teaching. But the experienced examiner knows that he must not indulge these preferences, if he is to be just. He must give fair play to men taught on other lines than his own. The easiest paper to set is often the hardest to mark. This is well known to old hands, who study how to spare themselves labour in marking by a little extra labour in setting. If you ask for the dates of half a dozen battles, you can mark the answers swiftly and surely. If you ask for the life and character of Cardinal Wolsey, you will not get off so easily. If you put a general question about the effect of the Reformation, you may get long answers, which require to be read and weighed, answers which will tax your patience and discrimination to the utmost. These general questions, though so hard to mark, are often the best of all. For ease of marking is not the chief thing which the examiner has to consider. The effect of his paper on the teaching of coming years is far more important. I have known a narrow and mechanical examiner, occupying an important post, to lower the standard of the teaching throughout the country. The examiner who puts easy and uniform marking in the first place inevitably favours routine-work. He favours grammar and discourages literature, favours dates and discourages history, favours the strong verbal memory and discourages the grasp of principles.

An examination paper should not be such that it could be handsomely answered by any candidate who had free use of a text-book. Papers of that sort, which are very common, encourage the verbal memory too much. But the dull, plodding candidate is not to be totally discouraged either. There should be a proportion of homely, straightforward questions on matters of fact.

It is a good plan to analyze the paper before sitting down to mark. Write out the points which ought to appear in the answers, and estimate their relative value. Subdivision is a great help to fair marking. After marking an answer in detail, run over it again, and try to form a general opinion as to its value. It is a good plan now and then to re-mark an old set of answers, and compare present and former results, as a test of the accuracy attainable. If the subject favours descriptive answers, the examiner will be lucky to keep within ten per cent. of deviation. Ten per cent. of accuracy is all that I claim myself; if I have to place a number of biological candidates I am satisfied if I can pretty certainly rank them according to ten degrees of merit, and then by a further scrutiny, place two or three of the best in order of merit. It is ridiculous to give out that we can recognize a hundred degrees of merit, yet this is implied in such an expression as 59 per cent. Over-precision in marking is a common and pernicious fallacy. For class-work there is nothing better than to arrange the names in four classes, answering to Excellent, Fair, Weak, and Hopeless. The excellents may then be placed in order of merit. I wish that some such method might drive out our misleading percentages.

A good and wholesome influence can only be exercised by an examiner who takes trouble. Trouble means time and money. If you cannot afford to pay a good man for taking pains, cease to examine. We could do very well with say half the present number of public examinations.

When I advocate reforms in teaching, I am often told of the necessity of meeting the requirements of certain examinations. The teacher will, however, be wise, even in his own interest, not to study the peculiarities of the examiner too closely. Teach your pupils, teach your subjects, and all will go well. It is true that you may be harassed at times by stupid questions. My students, for example, have to encounter questions which cannot be attempted except by those who know the pass-word. I will give a couple of specimens: (1) "What is meant by *holozoic* and *holophytic*? Give examples." (2) "What is meant by *concentric* and *collateral* bundles? Give examples." The examiner, misusing his position of advantage, insists upon a particular set of technical terms. I should think it base to get up those terms for next year's examination, unless I were satisfied that they are really helpful in teaching. Let my men pass or fail according as they have, or have not, a fair grasp of their subject; the examiner can usually be trusted to tell so much about them. Let us never, as teachers, allow the examiner to prescribe minutely what and how we are to teach. He is seldom fit for such a responsibility, being usually qualified only by knowledge and position, not by his familiarity with educational ideas; he is often an enemy to improvements.

Though we must not servilely defer to the examiner, it is legitimate and beneficial to train our pupils and students to express their meaning in a clear and connected manner. Show them how to methodize a complicated statement, how to make sure that they do not overlook a chief point. Careful drill in answering, both orally and in writing, pays better in examinations than the most anxious attention to dodges, and is of lasting benefit to the class.

A board of revision of examination papers and results seems to me absolutely required to check the vagaries of individual examiners. Unfortunately it is too often perfunctory, and fears to meddle with matters of expert knowledge. I have known one experienced member of such a board who caused the rewriting of a most unsuitable paper by pointedly asking the examiners who brought it up: "Why do you consider it important that the men should know this or that?" No good answer could be given; the examiners had not put such questions to themselves when they were setting their paper.

One of the chief improvements to fight for is the regular introduction of *vivâ voce* in conjunction with written papers. To follow up written answers by close questioning face to face with the candidate gives information otherwise unattainable. The mere written paper cannot, in most subjects, be trusted on an important occasion. Perhaps it may be trusted in Mathematics, Composition, and some other subjects, of which I have no practical experience. I am satisfied that in a modern language, any experimental or natural science, history or literature, a purely written examination is a most defective test.

I believe that examinations are useful and even indispensable. I also believe that far too much is made of them. No examination, nor any other piece of machinery, can sum up for us a man, with all his gifts and possibilities; yet it may tell us what he knows, and some little about what he can do. To let examinations prescribe the whole course of teaching and the early fate of every candidate is mischievous and cruel. Examinations, thus exalted to a dominant position, destroy the zeal of the teacher and the natural curiosity of the learner, injure the physical and mental health, and create false expectations of lasting success or failure. Examinations have their place, but it is a humble one; if we make the examiner master of the situation, we shall come to repent what we have done. Examinations are in their place when they test mere competence; they are more useful in lower than in higher stages; they should bring no rewards of money value either to pupil or teacher; they should count for little or nothing in the winning of posts. Professional merit is best judged by productive work. In a sound educational system the passing of an examination means little more than liberty to go on to the next stage.

A DIALOGUE ON PEDAGOGY AND PSYCHOLOGY.

[I have here tried the rather dangerous experiment of a dialogue, because it seemed to me that there were two sides to the question of the usefulness of pedagogy and psychology. I fancied that the arts professor had the best of the dispute, but the science professor was identified with myself, and I was held to have made an attack upon psychology. May I now speak a few words in my own person?

I believe that experimental psychology is not only a possible, but an actual science, and that the practical teacher will be more and more compelled to attend to it. As yet it is rather hopeful than useful, and the practical teacher not unnaturally treats the psychological lecturer of 1897 much as a grandmother would treat the little boy who, elated by a recent school-lesson on heat, should try to show her how to boil an egg. All the same, the future is on the side of scientific psychology.

There is also a paper-science of psychology, which goes much upon words and book-learning. I don't think it worth while to be told at length what A and B thought about the operations of the mind; let us know what they have proved.

We are as yet new to the business of training

teachers, and our methods are not so thorough as they ought to be. The teacher in training has often to struggle with a University course at the same time, and is therefore overworked; he listens to long courses of lectures on the theory of education; and his opportunities for practice in schools are insignificant. The teacher should be competent in general studies before he goes into training; if he is to graduate, he should graduate first. His training should be mainly given in the school. A lecturer on education without a school is, as I lately heard Mr. J. J. Findlay remark, like a science lecturer without a laboratory. One year of methodical training should be enough, if the ground has been properly prepared.

What is said of Bacon represents my settled opinion as to his place in scientific history. His distinction, which has endured for more than two centuries, is the distinction of a man of letters and affairs.

If I were to sum up the discussion in a few words, I should say that the science professor, though right on certain points of detail, is hasty and narrow. I have put into the mouth of the arts professor my deliberate convictions.]

    Sc. : A SCIENCE PROFESSOR.
    A. : AN ARTS PROFESSOR.

Sc. Look here! I want to show you part of an

article which I am writing. I have been slating the men who talk so big about the science of teaching, but I should like you or someone else to look over what I have said. I don't want to make an ass of myself, and I have read precious little of either theory of education or psychology.

A. Well, go on. I hope it is not very long.

Sc. (*Reads.*) "People who have views upon methods of teaching like to dignify them by the name of *Pedagogy*, which is taken to be an appropriate and agreeable designation for a science of education. Pedagogy, again, is supposed to rest upon psychology, which is the science of mental phenomena. Men of science who are not interested in the theory of education might demur to such names and to the ideas which are associated with them. They would deny that pedagogy is, or ever will be, a science at all. They would deny that the practical art of teaching need start from psychology. And lastly, many of them would refuse to admit that we have at the present time any adequate science of mental phenomena. Psychology will no doubt do great things in some remote future. But it is young and incompletely developed. A science should deal largely in experiment and observation, unless it is, like mathematics, concerned with the investigation of those numerical and geometrical laws which underlie all science. But the psychology of to-day is only experimental or observational in the most limited degree. It is in the main a collection of learned opinion, and has no means of enforcing its authority over those who make it their pastime to worry learned opinion, who love to make learned opinion either justify itself or give place to something which can. The course of science from Galileo's day to this has been on its critical side one incessant strife with learned opinion. Centuries of hard work, not of wordy discussion, are required to place psychology on the level which physiology has already attained. Meanwhile, its pretensions are far beyond its merits. Though it looks reasonable to insist upon a thoroughgoing knowledge of the mind of the child before you attempt to train that mind, it is fairly open to question whether a tolerable analysis of what goes on in the child's mind can be got by any process whatever. It is also a tenable proposition that unscientific common sense, the home-baked philosophy of experience, may be really a better guide to the teacher than the text-books of an immature science. The needful equipment of the teacher is common sense and experience. He will be all the better without those systems which usurp the name of science, while they are nothing more than the speculations of abstract thinkers."

A. It is easy to see that you have enjoyed

pitching into your opponents. But, to tell the truth, I am not quite sure who your opponents are.

Sc. Why, the exciting cause of my attack was the pompous talk of K. How I hate to hear him go on about the science of teaching, and Bacon, and the inductive method and all the rest! Why must every man claim to come in under science? If you turn over the pages of the *Academy* you may see a Greek play reviewed under the heading of science. It was not editors of Greek plays who made science a name to swear by! And Lord Bacon too! Bacon was nothing but a showy literary man, who attached himself to the most promising intellectual movement of his age. Any scientific man who looks into the *Novum Organum* will soon see how little Bacon knew of scientific investigation. His notion is to pile up particulars, and draw inferences from them by a mechanical method.

A. I must speak very guardedly on any question of scientific investigation, but is it not true that Bacon showed some practical sagacity in matters of science? I have heard people speak with enthusiasm of one passage in which he anticipated modern views about the nature of heat.

Sc. Yes, that is what everybody quotes. I admit, however, that he is entitled to score for that one passage. That it was a lucky guess is clear when we consider Bacon's treatment of the real science of his own day. He ignores Kepler, the Galilean mechanics, Napier's logarithms, Harvey's circulation of the blood; he definitely rejects the Copernican theory. His knowledge of heat was not in advance of his day, but behind it. Among natural sources of heat he reckons fur, feathers, and mustard. How little science owes either to Bacon or to the inductive philosophy! Joseph de Maistre is not far wrong when he says that those who have done most in science are those who have known least of Bacon.

A. Well, let Bacon rest in his grave. He suffers, like many another writer, from exaggerated praise. But if you had not been in a rage with K., I think you would hardly have said such strong things about pedagogy and psychology.

Sc. Very likely not. Do you know that the very word "pedagogy" is exasperating?

A. I dare say it is; but we shall get used to it in time. The other day I happened to look into a book on the English language written fifty years ago, and I was amused to find that the author, a man of good sense and good taste, had strong objections to the word "hand-book," which, it seems, was then a novelty. He wanted to keep to "manual." Sir James Fitzjames Stephen could not "endure the hideous adjective 'educational.'"

I suppose that neither "hand-book" nor "educational" sticks in any one's throat at present, and possibly "pedagogy" will be swallowed in time. I am not partial to it myself, but, surely, this is a small matter.

Sc. Of course it is, and I won't say any more about it. I have more serious objections to the phrase "science of teaching." Teaching is no science, but a practical art, like plumbing or weaving.

A. Or engineering? I notice that our College Calendar includes engineering among the sciences.

Sc. Yes, I don't object so much to that. Engineering has a theoretical basis, which is largely scientific. Engineering is mainly the working out of certain problems of machinery or construction, by the help of mathematics and physics. But the practical art of teaching has no sort of theoretical, much less of scientific, foundation. It is a question of mother-wit and experience.

A. You mean that a sensible man who devotes himself to teaching is sure to become a good teacher in time?

Sc. Yes, that is what I do mean.

A. And yet, both you and I know a man who has distinct talents for business, but is unspeakably dull as a teacher, in spite of a fairly long experience.

Sc. Oh! single cases will prove anything. I

know a man who has the theory of education at his fingers' ends, but no one will take him as an assistant-master.

A. I have no doubt that such cases are to be found. But please to observe that your argument is not quite logical. When I challenge your definition of a good teacher as insufficient, you retort by showing that another definition, which I have not used, is insufficient too.

Sc. Well, don't get too Socratic. What do you think we ought to require of the teacher, besides mother-wit and practice?

A. I should imagine that it would be well worth a teacher's while to discuss practical questions with another teacher. For instance, if a teacher is inclined to lock up a whole form on a Saturday afternoon, because some undiscovered rascal has put sugar into all the ink-wells, I should recommend a quiet discussion with his fellow-teachers. Again, it has happened to me to make great progress in practical teaching from seeing one first-rate lesson given. I shall never forget a certain lesson in solid geometry, which I attended as a visitor in a *Real-schule* in Dresden. And I practise, with advantage, almost every day of my life some practical hints which I got from Fitch's *Lectures on Teaching.* Here is one, not by any means one of the most important, but merely one of the briefest. "No single lesson should have many technical or unfamiliar terms in it; but every good lesson should, at least, introduce the learner to two or three new technical words, and make a distinct addition to his vocabulary. Every lesson, in fact, brings to light some name or formula which is specially characteristic of the new knowledge you are imparting, and will form a good centre, round which your recollections will cluster and arrange themselves after you have done. All such characteristic terms, names, and formulæ should be very distinctly written and underlined; special attention should be called to them, and *re*called at the end of the lesson; and the question may be asked, 'What use did we make of this word?'" Now, let me ask if it is not desirable to record such advances in the practical art of teaching as we make from time to time, whether by discussion, or example, or precept?

Sc. No doubt; that is plain common sense.

A. And I believe we should agree that such results of reflection and experience may be systematized, and set forth in books or lectures for the profit of young teachers.

Sc. Certainly; but let me make one remark here. The experience of another man is not so good as your own. The experience of a certain German teacher in the year 1790 is not so good or so impressive as the experience of a known and trusted colleague in the year 1890. Don't let us ever get very far from our base, that is, from the concrete experience of some individual teacher.

A. I am quite willing to adopt that phrase. Don't let us get far from our base. Montaigne says somewhere: "A man can never be wise but by *his own wisdom.*" We don't want to work by formulæ, which give in general terms the essence of experience that is not our own. But only a fool will refuse to learn from others. If we keep strictly to what we can learn from our own reflections on our own experience we shall become both narrow and mistaken. I might add to Montaigne's saying this other: "A man can never be wise *by his own wisdom alone.*" He must learn from all men, but only that which he makes *his own* will turn to profit.

Sc. That seems sound. Get notions where you can, and verify them by your own experience.

A. Every modest and painstaking teacher does that his whole life through. But don't let us attach exaggerated importance to mere experience. Some of the most mischievous teachers, unenlightened, unprogressive, and even brutal, have had experience enough. We want to liberalize experience. We want to open the teacher's mind, and help him to accept ideas from without. This can be done to some extent by helping him to

L

escape from his own narrow routine of practical duties. In fact, we want to train his imagination and sympathy and judgment so that he will be able to profit by ancient and remote experience, as well as by the experience which closely resembles his own. A good theory of education should help a teacher to get sound conclusions out of experiments which he has not made himself. At the same time, we must remember not to get too far from our base. Caution and modesty must be there to check paradox and extravagant generalization.

Sc. Theories of education seem to be so much in the air! The theorist upon a wide and complex subject like education is never checked by finding that his theories won't work. So he goes on dogmatizing, just because no one can prove that he is wrong.

A. It strikes me that if education were so exclusively a practical art, as you claimed just now, it ought to be easy to find the flaw in a mistaken theory of education. If the plumber has a mistaken theory about the circulation in a hot-water system, he soon finds out that it won't do.

Sc. That does not hold if the theory is detached from practice, and inapplicable to practice.

A. Of course not. But is the theory of education as taught in our colleges detached from practice? What I have seen of it does not incline me to share that belief. I think I could show, if I had a few hours to get up my case, that certain theorists on education, say Pestalozzi and Froebel, have acted very powerfully on practice. In fact, many of the founders of the theory of education were themselves practical teachers, and their theories sprang out of their own experience.

Sc. I know just enough of writers on education to see that you could make out a good enough case on that point. But let me try to make you see why some of us are so much inclined to rebel against the theories of the educationists. We find them claiming a position of authority; they assert, either in terms or implicitly, that education is their province, and that they are to be listened to as experts; they have invented their own technical language, and try to force this upon mankind. "Methodology" is a word like "pedagogy," which excites to revolt a practical teacher who is not a theorist.

A. I think you are very easily excited to revolt. What if this and that word is needless and pedantic? We must not decide a serious question on such trivial grounds. Every profession claims the right to its own technicalities, and, so far as I know, there is generally a fair, if not a complete, justification for them. To outsiders, the technical language, say of the musician or the chemist, is unintelligible, and therefore odious. I suppose that nothing gives such ready opportunity for jests as the technical language of any calling. But, if the technical language is really needed, it survives jesting.

Sc. Don't you think that some educational theorists go a good deal upon authority? I heard the other day what I should call a mistress of an infant school stand upon her dignity and say: "That is not according to the system—that is against Froebel's principles." What is the system?—what are Froebel's principles that they are not to be criticized?

A. You are giving up all that is worth discussion if you come down to the words of one individual teacher. Never mind whether they are wise or not. In any large profession there are plenty of people who will talk foolishly and arrogantly. But extravagances in language do not touch the theory of education. You and I know enough about teaching to agree that a teacher cannot be turned out by any mechanical method. Just now I am inclined to ask that the training of the teacher may be less technical and more human. Let us discourage the manufacture of teachers according to one pattern, and to this end let us recognize that there is more than one good way of training them. Initiation into the methods of a good school might be an ideal training, if accompanied by due explanation, and followed by a course of probation in which criticism and supervision were practised. But how shall the headmaster of a school of high repute, who is one of the busiest of mortals, undertake so laborious a task? It inevitably gravitates to the specialist, and we must pray that the specialist will not worship his own position too much. May it never come about that teachers in training fall into the hands of lecturers who insist upon a pedantic method!

Sc. I am so far convinced as to admit the possibility of useful instruction in ways of teaching. "Theory of Education" I dislike; "Science of Education" I protest against as misleading; "Pedagogy" I hate and abominate.

A. You have granted all that I care about. But I should like to take up your remarks on psychology. Do you totally disbelieve in the possibility of a science of mind?

Sc. Well, that is going far. But I believe that it is one of the least developed of the sciences, and I should like to make it take a back seat.

A. That is clear from your article. But let us follow the question a little further. You will agree with me that certain observant people, not a few of them conversant with medicine, physiology, or some other branch of science which you respect, have got together a good deal of valuable information concerning the action of mind in health and disease. Insanity, Mental Fatigue, Memory, are headings which will remind you of the kind of observations I am thinking of. Is it not well to record and systematize such observations?

Sc. Of course it is.

A. And to extend them and communicate them?

Sc. Yes.

A. A considerable body of experiment and observation on mental phenomena is surely entitled to rank as a science of mind?

Sc. Yes; but there is so little experiment or observation, and so much of what I call learned opinion.

A. Too much, I dare say. But it is surely good for the teacher to know something of the results of psychological experiment and observation, if only to fix his attention upon what goes on in the mind of the child whom he is teaching?

Sc. I am not at all sure that I can agree with you. An inadequate and immature science may be worse than nothing, if it is the guide of men who think it more complete than it really is. I have seen a man give himself such airs, on the ground of a three-months' course of psychology, that he made me long to put him through some stiff mathematical reading in a good class. That would soon take the conceit out of him!

A. To take the conceit out of people is a mission that you take to very kindly. But it can hardly be a property essential to psychology that it lends itself so easily to imposture and pretence.

Sc. Any bookish science offers special opportunities for imposture and pretence.

A. Somehow or other I have never happened to find pretenders who carried on their career by the help of psychology, though cases are common in which men trade upon their pretended knowledge of medicine, electricity, and chemistry.

Sc. What do you say about my contention that psychology is, if a science at all, an undeveloped science?

A. The best exponents of psychology would admit that. They do not try to conceal the fact that psychology has still a great part of its work unaccomplished. Wundt and James tell you, as candidly as can be wished, that the experimental side of psychology is quite in its infancy. They would, however, claim that psychology has accumulated a good deal of positive knowledge, due to methods which are either not experimental, or not purely so. But why do you insist so much upon the undeveloped state of psychology? It is not so undeveloped as chemistry was in Robert Boyle's time, and you would not have been careful to disparage that, had you been, say, one of the founders of the Royal Society.

Let me remind you that Socrates, as reported by Xenophon, held that we should never know anything to signify about the causes of natural phenomena. They were, he thought, too capricious, governed immediately by the will of the gods, and could not be explained or predicted. Locke saw reason for supposing that we should never have a philosophy of Nature, because the works of Nature are "too far surpassing our faculties to discover or capacities to conceive." These "follies of the wise" should warn us not to despair, but to go on trying.

Sc. I wish you would justify psychology more directly by showing what it has done.

A. That is a hard task to put upon any man suddenly. But think of the work which has been done in such subjects as Habit, Attention, Association, Memory, Sensation, and Instinct. Remember that men like Darwin and Galton (to give only names which you cannot affect to despise) have thought these subjects worth their time and thought. Insanity and the treatment of insanity owe a great deal to psychology. So does education, but I will not press that point just now, as it is part of the question we are considering. What I have said goes to defend psychology against those who see no good in it rather than to prove that it is of special value to the teacher. But I believe that too. I believe that we have a considerable body of solid and useful information respecting such matters as the way in which we acquire knowledge, the order of intellectual progress, and other things of the greatest possible value to teachers. Unfortunately I cannot exemplify what I say without treating you to more psychology than you would care for. Psychology, taught solidly and in a practical way, is just that subject on which a body of intending teachers can usefully specialize. They cannot agree to study chemistry or botany, in which many of them have no particular interest. But I will agree that chemistry or botany, together with a practical course in what, with your permission, we will call pedagogy, would do very well as equipment for a special kind of teacher. I partly share your aversion to the systematic exposition of learned opinion on abstract subjects. The treatises on psychology give us too much of that. I often long to see a new elementary text-book of psychology. It should be written by a man who is quite at home in experimental physiology. It should treat simply and without "learned nimbus" of those mental qualities and operations which concern practice, and especially the practice of teachers. It should be plain, concise, and interesting, suited to stimulate reflection and observation. Sir John Herschel's *Study of*

Natural Philosophy, though it relates to another subject, shows the kind of book I mean. Well-ascertained facts applied copiously to the elucidation of important questions sufficiently describes the method of that excellent book. I wish we had a whole library of such on subjects of all kinds.

Sc. There is not much left for us to discuss. I am very glad to have daylight let into the dark places of my own mind. Something of the old Adam still struggles within me, however, when I think of the dogmatic opinions laid down upon these subjects by men who never made an experiment or an observation for themselves.

A. I am afraid that we cannot apply an instant remedy to all folly. But psychology is not more to blame than other sciences. It is only when the conception and essential methods of a science are faulty that it must bear the sins of its professors. You and I know of one man who cannot lecture on chemical combination without rousing something of a rebellious spirit—so hard, so pedantic, is his manner. Dogmatism and pedantry are always bad, but not, I think, either more common or more odious among psychologists than among other people.

Sc. I think I will twist up my manuscript for pipe-lights.

A. It would be better to keep it, and add

the reasons which now make you think it a little one-sided.

Sc. I think it would clear up my own thoughts if I were to try. I will write down what occurs to me, in the form of a dialogue between an Arts man and a Science man on Pedagogy and Psychology.

THE TRAINING OF A GREAT NATURALIST.

My subject is K. E. von Baer, known to the scientific world as an embryologist, a naturalist, a geographer, and an ethnologist. The materials for this short study are drawn from his own writings, and especially from an autobiographical sketch, "Leben und Schriften von K. E. von Baer," written in old age.

Baer was born in 1792 in the Baltic province of Esthonia. Though nominally a Russian, his family and name were German. His father was a small landed proprietor. Baer learnt the first elements from a capable domestic tutor, named Steingrüber. Under him the boy went through a pretty extensive course of mathematics. His progress was rapid, for he was able to take up plane trigonometry at ten. Steingrüber paid much attention to the practical applications of mathematical theory, and taught, among other things, the elements of surveying, so that Baer, when a boy of eleven, was able to show his father a measured plan of the family domain with all its houses and trees. Geography was another principal study, and here again the practical bent of the teacher showed itself. The children were made to trace and colour maps, until they completed a school atlas of their own. French was taught carefully, Latin kept back later than usual. One admirable feature of Steingrüber's teaching was the restriction of the school hours to five a day, which were made to include all the school exercises. There were two half-holidays in the week, no occasional holidays of any kind, and very short terminal holidays.

Baer dwells with pleasure upon the gardening which occupied much of his leisure in summer, upon a Babylonian tower with winding walks, which he and his brothers made with spade and barrow, upon the skating and sleighing of mid-winter, and upon the paper-cutting and map-drawing which were the indoor-amusements of the long winter evenings. "All this," says he, "was perfectly good." There was but one drawback to their happiness, and that was the increasing lack of companions. Training for military service carried off the boys of the neighbouring estates at an age when they ought to have been making Babylonian towers and cutting out paper, and at last the children who were left were too few to play heartily. Baer's father was wise enough to send his boys to school late, and to keep them there longer than usual.

Of this father and of his influence upon the character of his children, Baer speaks with gratitude and respect. He was a sober and diligent man of business, who rose every morning at four to look after his farm. His turn of mind was mechanical, but he had studied law, and held some official appointments. He was the favourite executor in the province, and guardian to many fatherless children. He spent much of his leisure in reading, but not for pleasure, nor altogether for profit. Romances, with the exception of Scott's, were his aversion. He had little literary curiosity, and took no pains to remember what he read. When an old man he found a popular Encyclopædia or Conversations-Lexicon to be the sort of reading which suited him exactly, and he read it steadily through. With his children he was grave, not easily provoked, and never peevish.

Baer's father was an agricultural innovator, and made some trouble for himself by pressing reforms upon the peasants of his estate. It is curious to note what these reforms were, the time spoken of being the years 1800-4. Clover-growing, the cutting of turf for fuel, and the use of potatoes for human food were the new-fangled inventions which the peasantry could not abide. Thirty years before, Frederick the Great had met with the same difficulties in Silesia. "We won't eat roots," said the German peasants, and the official answer was: "No one wants you to eat them, but you must grow them. The King will eat them himself." Baer's father made his people take from him a given quantity of potatoes every spring, and bring as much back in autumn. The peasants, it is to be remarked, were then serfs, the first act of partial emancipation dating from 1804. Of his mother, Baer says that she was a quiet housewife and an affectionate parent, who liked her acts of kindness to pass without word spoken.

When Baer was eleven, a new tutor, Glanström, replaced Steingrüber. Glanström had studied science, and particularly medicine; he had much skill in modern languages, and was also a musician. Of mathematics and drawing, which had been strong points in his predecessor, he had no special knowledge. Baer now worked hard at his languages—French, Latin, English, and some Italian, in addition to his native German. Glanström was not so careful and assiduous as his predecessor, and the two elder boys were now left to do much of their work alone. They were looked upon as sufficiently advanced to help the younger children, and Baer, at the age of twelve, was set to teach geography to a little sister of seven. So earnestly did he enter upon his work, that he prepared a text-book of his own whose chief merit, says the Autobiography, was its extreme brevity. Now for the first time the study of Nature attracts the boy's mind. One day he found the tutor with a book in one hand and some flowers in the other. Asking what this meant, he was told that the book gave the names of all the flowers. Young Baer could not rest till he had got such a book for his own, and without teacher, for the tutor knew no more than himself, he began to collect and determine all the plants of the district. The garden and even the Babylonian tower were now neglected, and the herbarium grew apace. Snakes, lizards, fossils, and every kind of natural object were in time added to the collection.

When Baer was fifteen, his father thought fit to send him to the public school at Reval. The boy had already mastered French and English, could read Latin fairly, and was forward in mathematics. He knew no Greek, and his knowledge of history was drawn entirely from an old-fashioned text-book, of which the first volume was missing. Such attainments sufficed to place him in the highest form, except for Greek.

Baer praises his school as efficient and of good tone, and declares that the very happiest years of his life were spent there. The headmasters were Wehrmann, a pupil of Heyne's, and the mathematician Blasche. Of Wehrmann's industry and management he speaks in the warmest terms. When a scholar of the highest form was put on to read, and was found unprepared, which occasionally but rarely happened, no word of blame was needed. The look of reproach and the call to the next student to take the passage were punishment enough. Baer got at Reval a facility of reading Latin and Greek, which was a source of delight to him throughout his whole life. Years after, when his great scientific labours were ended, he was able to occupy his leisure with those remarkable essays, entitled "Historical Questions answered by means of Scientific Research," writings which exhibit a detailed knowledge, not only of the coasts and rivers and headlands, but of the poets, geographers, and historians, of Greece and Rome. Baer naturally asks why the schoolmaster should exercise his pupils, who, as a rule, can read no ancient author with accuracy and ease, in the most difficult parts of difficult authors. At the University he afterwards became intimate with a student brought up in the gymnasium of Königsberg, under a master who was said to believe that no man had a right to enjoy the sunshine who was not a competent classic. The young man bore the special certificate of classical proficiency, but Baer was amused to find that he could not read ordinary Latin for want of a vocabulary. When he asked again and again, "What does that word mean?" Baer was driven to exclaim, "Is it possible that you don't know?"

The mathematical teaching at Reval must have been very respectable. Baer relates that Blasche once told his class that the times of sunrise and sunset given in the Reval Nautical Almanac had not been recalculated for some years, and he proposed to them that they should undertake it as a holiday exercise. The results were got and printed next year in the Reval Almanac. The physics course lasted over several years, and must have been fairly thorough.

Baer tells us that his school work was moderate in amount, that he and the rest worked without hurry or anxiety. He found time for botanical rambles, for pretty extensive reading in the light literature of England and Germany, and also for a little club, held in turn at the houses of some of his school-fellows. The boys began with the solid part of their entertainment, which consisted of Greek or Latin. Afterwards came German poetry, then tea, and, if fortune was kind, a dance with the young ladies of the house. Things had changed for the worse by the time that Baer sent his own boys to school in St. Petersburg. They had to work late, writing out pages of Latin exercises, and begged to be called early in the morning to finish their tasks. "It is very well," says Baer, "to know precisely how often Sylla and Marius were consuls, but even this knowledge may be bought too dear."

Baer's thirst for knowledge may be judged of by a little anecdote which belongs to his school-days. A book auction was held in the town, and Baer turned over the books. He found Hederic's Lexicon, which seemed to him a treasure, because it gave not only all words of classical authority, but also all the mediæval and modern Latin used in books of philosophy, medicine, chemistry, and astronomy. This invaluable book he must needs have. An Arabic book next tempted him, then a bundle of printed papers in a language which the auctioneer did not venture to name. The bundle proved to be a collection of Icelandic Sagas. All these, together with four volumes of a mathematical treatise, and an English text-book of medicine, the schoolboy carried off with delight. He had to pay for them with his whole stock of pocket-money, and this was no slight sacrifice. Breakfast at school consisted simply of a hard cake or biscuit, without butter or drink of any kind. The boys were accustomed to mend their cheer with milk, for which they paid out of their own pockets. Now that all his cash had gone in books, Baer had a dry biscuit every morning, and nothing more. But the thought of his invaluable Lexicon sweetened this untempting fare, and, after eating it cheerfully for a few weeks, the young

Spartan disdained to go back to milk and sweets, although times had mended. The Lexicon he kept and used throughout his long life. Whenever he moved to a new city or a new country, and he sometimes moved so far that his library had to be left behind, he never failed to take Hederic's Lexicon with him.

There were, of course, weak points in this as in every other school. Baer says that the teaching of Russian, the language of the State, was inadequate and unintelligent. Instead of giving the boys the best native literature to read, a compendium of history, chiefly ancient, with moral reflections, was made the text-book. The Latin names bothered the teacher, who, as the boys soon found out, knew nothing but the Russian which he taught. When they came upon the common contraction L. for Lucius, the boys must needs pretend not to know what it meant. Did it perhaps stand for Ludwig or Leopold? The teacher weakly thought that it might, and after this, there was no end to the traps which they laid for him. Baer, who was no doubt one of the tormentors, had the tables turned upon him in the end, for, though he spent the last forty years of his life in Russia, and had to write and lecture in Russian, he never got easy command of the language. He thinks further that too special subjects, such as Hebrew, jurisprudence, and fortification, were taught in the school, subjects imposed by unwise directors, who were too strongly impressed with the necessity of exercising the future divine, lawyer, or soldier at the earliest possible age in the fundamental studies of his profession. Baer discusses the relative merits of the humanist course, based upon classical learning, and the realist, based upon subjects of every-day utility, but declines to accept either as the one true method. He wants discipline above all, and this he finds in the study of the ancient languages. He does not dispute the claim of certain teachers, now reputed a little old-fashioned, who declare that the thorough grounding of the Gymnasium is an excellent preparation for studies which are never admitted there. But he does not think that mental gymnastic is to be got in no other way, nor does he think that there is any magical virtue in the classics, taught carelessly or by rote. Miscellaneous information about camels and cocoa-palms, clouds and burning mountains, the Philanthropinismus of Basedow, he would provide by means of entertaining books read out of school. He does not value early specialism, and discourages distinct courses of school education adapted to the future calling of the scholars. Yet he will not have the future calling overlooked either. He derides the schoolmaster who, on the ground that they must first be made into men, and then taught useful knowledge, tried to persuade him that his own boys need not learn Russian, the language of the State.

Baer is not enough of a theorist for those who like sharp-cut and even paradoxical views. When he has said something smartly, he often takes away the effect by pointing out considerations which tell on the other side. One moment he is fighting the advocates of one particular kind of perversity, and the next he deals a blow at their opponents. What has proved sound in his own career is the thing that he believes in above all.

Classical studies he thinks admirable, if the best is made of them. The exact sciences, too, he values highly as school subjects. Of his own school, where these two were dominant, he says that it did for him all that a school could do. At the same time he gladly recognizes the usefulness of the descriptive sciences in making children observant and active.

The teaching must be human, calling forth the powers which lie dormant in the child. "A human being," he says in one very Froebelian passage, "is not to be treated as dough, ready to take any shape which may be impressed upon it; it contains germs to be nourished and fostered."

"The teacher should not only know and love his *Fach*" (how is this word to be translated?

Subject, which is common, is inaccurate and sometimes impossible), "but should have pondered upon methods of instruction, and be well practised in them. Such men are still rare among us."

"The great Linnaeus took so little interest in his Hebrew at school, being absorbed in out-of-door Nature, that he was near being sent home as incorrigible. His father, finding him so dull in intellectual things, thought of making a shoemaker of the boy. Many a human life is ruined because too narrow a road is marked out for it to run in. Thus the character becomes crushed or distorted. And yet what a man accomplishes in the course of his life depends mainly upon his character—more upon what he *is* than upon what he *knows*."

One other remark we must not omit to quote. He speaks of his school-fellows with respect and gratitude, and says that it was good for him that the almost solitary home-lessons were replaced at the right time by the stirring emulation of the class-room. The companionship of his school-fellows made what he calls the poetical element of these boyish days.

In 1810, Baer, then a young man of eighteen, entered the University of Dorpat as a student of Medicine. The choice of this University was not, in his mature opinion, a good one. Dorpat was very new, founded only eight years before Baer entered, and ill-furnished with resources, whether material or intellectual. The little town, which had no trade to speak of, and largely subsisted by help of the University, could give no stimulus of its own. This leads Baer to observe that a University should never be planted in a very small place. The supposed advantages of seclusion and frequent intercourse with the professors are useless to students who have none of the enthusiasm and ambition created by numbers, and who run together, as they did at Dorpat, for all kinds of trivial and childish purposes. Baer thinks that the University should never constitute more than one influence among the many which must co-operate to make a well-equipped man, and that the student should have many points of contact with men engaged in active business, as well as with family life. Years after, when he came to read Goethe's Autobiography, it struck Baer that his own student days had been without opportunity of intimate association with men of rich experience and impressive character. He would have the University removed to Riga, a great seaport, for the sake of a varied and imposing social element. He adds that in the last years of his studies it is of the greatest value to the student that he should carry on his work in a great capital, range over vast collections, enjoy opportunities of becoming known to the leaders of his own profession, and be set free from close supervision of his work. To a medical student the insignificance of the town of Dorpat was a serious disadvantage, for it had no large hospitals, and the teaching was largely bookish.

Among the professors were some men of mark, the physicist Parrot, the botanist Ledebour, and the physiologist Burdach. But the good elements in the University were crushed by poverty and officialism. The teaching appliances were miserable, the staff so inadequate that each professor had to undertake extra subjects beyond those which he had specially studied. Baer tells in amusing detail how some of the subjects were taught. The lectures on anatomy, for example, were given by a certain Professor Cichorius, who appeared in a long, close-buttoned, official uniform, and solemnly delivered his lectures with what Baer calls a grudging outlay of useful matter. In a singing tone he read through these dreary discourses, which were varied only by questions supposed to be put by a hearer thirsting for information: "Where now is this gland situated?" —"It is situated between—— and——." Or, as the attention of the class visibly drooped, he would from time to time warn them that what he taught he taught in the name of the Czar. Cichorius was outwardly diligent, lecturing six hours a week upon osteology alone, but empty and unworthy of respect. It was one of his whims to sit all day by candle light, with the shutters up. Another less innocent peculiarity was a love of strong drink, and the air of his lecture room was flavoured by alcoholic fumes.

Then there was a Lecturer on Methodology and the History of Medicine, who began by setting forth the requirements of the study. First, the medical student must be proficient in Latin, because all prescriptions are written in Latin. Next, he must know Greek, for Hippocrates and Galen wrote in Greek. Lastly, Arabic was needful, because Rhazes and Avicenna wrote in Arabic. After these conditions had been laid down and justified, the lecturer deferred what he had further to say upon methodology and the history of medicine, and went on with routine hospital work. Baer says, bitterly enough, that the professors of Dorpat sought to invest themselves with a nimbus of learning, like the glory round the head of a painted saint. Instead of explaining, simply and out of their own experience, the characters of various diseases, they read out the titles of a number of books, and students who did not know how to let blood were lectured upon the state of medicine under the Pharaohs.

It was a sad time for Baer. He managed to learn something by hospital attendance. He kept up his botany, too, and Ledebour, the botanical professor, was of use to him. But as for anatomy, there was not even the possibility of dissection. Years after, in Würzburg, Baer had to take out a course of practical anatomy, because he had not the skill in dissection necessary for the comparative anatomy on which he was bent.

Two years after Baer's entrance upon medical studies at Dorpat came the invasion of Russia by Napoleon. General Macdonald besieged Riga, and the Russian army within the city soon came to want extra medical assistance. The neighbouring University was appealed to, and twenty-five young students volunteered for hospital service in Riga. Twenty-four of the number were immediately struck down by typhus, and Baer was one of these. He lay in his lodging, unvisited, except that once a day the daughter of the house looked in to see whether he was ready to be carried off on a bier, and unsupplied, except with a flask of vinegar and water, which stood by the bed. After some days the fever abated, and youthful strength prevailed. Baer had made an involuntary, but favourable, trial of the expectant method. As soon as he recovered, he went back to duty, and indeed there was need of helpers, for the hospital was crowded to excess. New comers lay for three days in an unwarmed room, though it was frosty weather, and Baer's share of the patients numbered 150. To give each patient five minutes meant more than twelve hours' work daily. Happily, the French were soon in full retreat, and Riga got clear of the war. "It is very uncertain," says Baer, "whether we students from Dorpat were able to render the State much service."

At last, in 1814, Baer was ready to be examined for his degree. His professional knowledge was poor indeed, but the examination was adapted to the course of study. First came Anatomy. Baer had seen some of the parts demonstrated, and had done what he could by reading, but he knew only too well how inadequate his preparation had been. "I will not say," are his own words, "that Nature has made anything in vain, but for a poor medical student, who has to take up at once all the bones, ligaments, tendons, muscles, nerves, vessels, and viscera, besides Physics, Chemistry, Zoology, Botany, Materia Medica, Pathology, and the rest, there are certainly too many parts in the human body." In Physiology the candidate was asked: "How many types of organization are there?" Cuvier or Meckel, he adds, would have been puzzled to answer, but those who had attended Cichorius' lectures knew that there were two only, the fluid and the imperfectly fluid. Medusæ or jelly-fish were cited as examples of the completely fluid type.

After the examination came the dissertation. Baer wrote upon "The Epidemic Diseases of

Esthonia," and his thesis had, he says, about as much value as other productions by young people of no experience, that is to say, very little value indeed.

The dissertation was printed, and only one formality remained. The diploma required that the candidate should have performed one of the major operations upon the dead body before examiners. But no dead body was to be had. The vacation came, the new term began—still no body! Inquiry brought to light in the military hospital a patient who, as the hospital physician good-naturedly predicted, would be dead in a couple of days. Allowing a margin of four days, the 24th of August was fixed for the operation, but on the 24th the man was still alive. The delay became irksome, for Baer had arranged to travel with other students through Germany, and his companions were now waiting only for him. On the 29th the patient actually died. Baer cut off his leg, and was made Doctor of Medicine on the spot. Fifty years later that day was celebrated by a public festival of the gentry of Baer's native province, and to preserve a lasting memorial of the festival, he was persuaded to write the Autobiography from which I have drawn the story of his early life.

"I was now," he says, "*doctor medicinae rite promotus*, but had little trust in my own skill, and not much in medicine. Had any sick man asked me to recommend a physician, I should have bidden him choose whom he would, so long as he did not choose me." People told him that in Vienna there were great hospitals, and that much was to be learnt from Hildenbrand, who had just published a work on Typhus. So to Vienna Baer proceeded. He gave himself seriously to hospital work in medicine and surgery, and found good instruction as well as plenty of cases. But as his opportunities grew, it became more and more clear to Baer's mind that he was not fit for medical practice. The mountains not far from Vienna tempted him to botanize once more, and he found it hard to go back from his rambles to hospital routine. He thought of teaching botany for a living; but in the Baltic provinces, where his hopes of promotion lay, there was but one chair of Botany, and that was now occupied. Zoology was equally attractive, but here too there was no present opening. Moreover good instruction in natural history was not to be had, even if there had been the prospect of ultimate preferment. The new studies of geology and comparative anatomy rose before him like ranges of distant mountains, unknown but fascinating. All these dreams, these longings for congenial work, had as yet no practical possibility for the young doctor of medicine. Time after time, he broke away from hospital practice to delight himself with natural history, but always in the end repressed the rash impulse, and forced his mind to run in the groove of practical medicine. Baer's uncertainty at this time, and his distraction between professional duty and natural bent, remind us of the sad history of Swammerdam. Brought up, like Baer, to medical practice, Swammerdam had an irresistible inclination towards natural history. No prospect of ease and independence, no arguments of the severe father who threatened to disinherit him, could divert his passionate curiosity. He pressed on to explore the secrets of Nature in spite of obstacles which broke his health and ruined his happiness. Baer's struggles were less disastrous. The love of Nature was in him predominant, but not tyrannical; father and friends were considerate and helpful. In the end Baer became a naturalist and not a physician, but he never, like Swammerdam, cast off his early studies as a hateful burden. Human anatomy and physiology helped to realize his true vocation, and the schools of medicine gave him necessary help and maintenance until he had made himself a master in those pursuits towards which he was drawn by a gentle but irresistible destiny.

A little incident, which at the time seemed absolutely trivial, proved to be the turning point in Baer's career. While making a botanical excursion on the Schneeberg, he fell in with two strangers, one the well-known botanist, Hoppe, the other a young man, afterwards to be widely celebrated as Martius, the traveller and illustrator of palms. Talking together, Baer happened to mention that he was about to visit Würzburg for the sake of hospital practice. Martius, who had just ended his studies at Würzburg, begged him to take charge of a packet of mosses which he wished to send to Döllinger. "Certainly," said Baer, "but who is Döllinger?"—"An anatomist, who can give you instruction in comparative anatomy, if you want it." This chance remark excited Baer's hopes. Instruction in comparative anatomy was precisely what he did want, and not many days later, he introduced himself to Döllinger, handed to him Martius' packet of mosses, and explained that he had himself come to Würzburg to attend the course of lectures in comparative anatomy. "But I don't lecture on comparative anatomy this term," was the answer. Baer stood perplexed, with the bottom knocked out of his plans. Then Döllinger at length went on: "What do you want with lectures? Bring me any animals you please, first one and then another, and dissect them here." Next morning, Baer brought a leech to Döllinger, who showed him what instruments to buy, how to kill the leech, and how to prepare it for dissection under water. Slowly and clumsily the work went on. When it was finished, Döllinger brought out Spix's beautiful memoir on the Leech, and gave it to Baer to study at home. Now Baer saw what was to be done, and returned to his leech with fresh interest. Other types were taken up, one after another, in the same way. Döllinger was at hand to explain points of unusual difficulty, but in general he went on with his own work, mounting his mosses, or examining them under the microscope. Baer tells us that before he had worked under Döllinger for a fortnight he felt that he was in the right path, and day by day he could see distinct progress, some new fact gained, some new method practised. All the doubts as to what and where he should study were dispelled. Now he knew what he was fit for, and was content to let the future shape itself.

Döllinger's methods were then new in the world. They originated in his own simple and practical character. It was usual during Baer's student-time to lecture profusely. The Professor of Zoology lectured upon the classes and orders of the animal kingdom. If more detail was wanted, he lectured upon genera and species. Döllinger swept all this aside, and went straight to the real point. The student was to work for himself, to work under direction, but actively and responsibly. A fresh set of difficulties now come in, but they are difficulties worth facing. Young men gradually learn to be careful and systematic, to trust their own eyes, to walk without leading-strings. There is no longer set before them the endless task of getting up all that the books have to teach, but the hope of gaining new results by practising well-tried methods. Döllinger's teaching, if faithfully carried out, takes the young biologist into the very heart of his subject.

In our own time and country, the same method of teaching biology has been practised with eminent success by Professor Huxley. I do not know whether or not he learnt it from Döllinger, but it was Döllinger who first showed that the study of concrete animal types is a necessary preliminary to any really good work in zoology or comparative anatomy. If you teach comparative anatomy, don't begin with the theory of the skull, or any sort of abstraction. If you teach botany, don't begin with the homology of the parts of the flower. First, observation and practice; afterwards reflection and theory.

One thing which is related concerning Döllinger's lectures is thoroughly characteristic. He hated all preludes, introductions, trivial facts, quotations, and what Baer calls "learned nimbus." The essential points were explained till they were clear as sunlight, and all the rest was passed by without spoken word.

Döllinger, says Baer, was, first and last, a teacher. It seemed to him no part of his work to win fame for himself. He would hand over to a good student any really great opportunity of research which came in his way. It was his delight to have students about him at home; some of them lived with him, and worked in his own study. If a student was very poor, Döllinger contrived to find food and lodging for him; if he was rich, Döllinger instigated him to set about some piece of work which required outlay of money. To those who know anything of the recent history of biology, it is enough to say that Döllinger trained Purkinje, Pander, Martius, Baer, and Agassiz. No words of ours can add to this praise, nor can any teacher desire a nobler epitaph than Baer's respectful and affectionate tribute.[1]

The work which Baer, by Döllinger's advice, at length set himself to accomplish was to trace more completely than his predecessors the development of the chick. I need not explain in how masterly a way the task was performed. Baer now became a teacher and an investigator, and his labours pass beyond the grasp of a sketch like this.

---

[1] It may interest some readers to know that J. J. Ignaz Döllinger, the leader of the Old Catholics, was a son of that Döllinger who taught Baer.

I will merely make one extract more, which shows how he set about teaching anatomy when appointed assistant to Burdach at Königsberg.

He had himself studied anatomy in three Universities. In Würzburg, and later in Berlin, he had been taught practical anatomy on two different systems. At Würzburg much stress had been laid upon the style of the work. All the dissections were made with an eye to class demonstrations, and were often preserved permanently by the students of the school. Few of the men worked through any considerable part of human anatomy, and none were obliged to do more than look on. Demonstrations were given, and these were carefully done, but most of the students took no part in them. Baer thought that here all was sacrificed to perfecting the technical skill of the few who desired to excel. He thought, and Döllinger thought too, that teaching was put on one side for the sake of perfection in a mechanical operation.

At Berlin the students were left to manage their own dissections without supervision. The Professor or Demonstrator appeared twice a day, and was at once beset by students seeking help in their work. From this molestation he escaped as soon as possible. Under this system there was a certain eagerness to learn anatomy, but to learn it with the smallest possible expenditure of time.

The handbook upon which the student entirely depended was read diligently, and a rough method of mutual help was organized. The older students walked about the room to see as much as they could without working for themselves, and in return they gave hints to the beginners. All the work was done carelessly, and in a small fraction of the time which it ought to have occupied.

Baer could not adopt either of these methods. One aimed at nothing but technical skill; the other neglected technical skill altogether. One prescribed a course too laborious for any but the most docile; the other left every student at liberty to teach himself. Baer made it a duty to attend constantly in the dissecting-room, and to see that every dissector had necessary help and supervision. But the responsibility of the student was not interfered with. Instead of looking on while somebody demonstrated, the student had to demonstrate all the essential points, on his own preparation, to Baer himself. This plan, in which the practical good sense of Döllinger shows itself, worked well in practice, and Baer had the satisfaction of turning out some good anatomists. Five future professors were among his students in this small school of Königsberg, and one at least of these (Reichert) attained a European reputation.

Here we must leave our great naturalist. He

has shown us as well as he could how to learn and how to teach. The practical lessons to be drawn from the rest of the Autobiography relate to the art of investigation, and not to the art of teaching.

THE EDGEWORTHS ON PRACTICAL EDUCATION.

A hundred years ago there was a well-to-do family of uncommon intelligence and enterprise, which had made the education of its children a principal care. The children gave plenty of practice, for there were, from first to last, eighteen of them, by four mothers; and when the youngest was one year old the eldest had passed forty-five. The father, Richard Lovell Edgeworth, was an active, observant man, with a natural turn for experiment. He had worked at the telegraph of those days, which we now call a semaphore, and had transmitted verses, written for the occasion, across the narrowest part of the channel between Ireland and Scotland, in the presence of an admiring crowd. He had contrived a "perambulator," which he afterwards called an "odometer," that is, a way-measuring wheel. He had experimented on wheeled carriages, and had made a journey in a one-wheeled carriage of his own, a kind of horse-wheelbarrow, excellent for narrow roads and bridges. He had helped to divert the Rhone at Lyons, and thereby to recover a tract of land valuable for its neighbourhood to the city. After trying several places of residence in the course of his rather unsettled life, Mr. Edgeworth had now established himself on his own estate in the heart of Ireland. Here he occupied himself with the better management of his leases, with the drainage of bogs, with public affairs (for he was elected to the last Irish Parliament), with the Board of Education, and with philanthropic schemes for the benefit of his people. He had an eye to the humours of the Irish peasantry, and, in concert with his eldest daughter, Maria Edgeworth, wrote a treatise on Irish Bulls, which, though liable to be mistaken for a practical guide to stock-raising, was in reality an excellent collection of odd sayings.

Edgeworth's second wife was an English lady, Honora Sneyd, who showed her good sense and originality by the notes which she made of her children's conversation. She seems to have had plans of education of her own, and to have recorded the results, though it is not easy to say for certain whether she got the notion from her husband or gave it to him. The scientific spirit in which Mrs. Edgeworth worked may have been inspired by the society of her native city of Lichfield, where Watt, Priestley, Wedgwood, and

Erasmus Darwin had long been familiar figures. With that society, however, both husband and wife had been intimate. Mr. Edgeworth knew the Lichfield and Birmingham set, and kept up a correspondence with Erasmus Darwin in particular. The eldest daughter of the family was the celebrated novelist, Maria Edgeworth, a shrewd and amiable woman, who won the respect and liking of Sir Walter Scott and many other excellent judges.

We can imagine what the tea-table talks at Edgeworthstown were like—how familiar the chief writers of England and France were to that little company; how science and its practical applications were valued; how keen was the appreciation of a humorous trait; how lively the interest in the developing intelligence of the little ones! The Edgeworths were never Boswellized, but they wrote down in a book what we may take to be the cream of their conversation. That book is "Practical Education," by Maria and R. L. Edgeworth. If the reader should light upon that ancient book, he will do well to read it, for it contains authentic histories of the thoughts of children. Judges of human character, so observant and so sympathetic as the Edgeworths, were not likely, we might well suppose, to pass over the child in training, and to treat the workings of his mind as if they were only ill-learned lessons. And yet this was the habit of writers on education, both then and since. The subject and the method were taken to be all in all. The child's mind was a thing which could not indeed be left out of consideration, but it was regarded as a thing to be shaped and guided. The more accurately it took the form prescribed, the better for all concerned, and this form was, of course, to be found in the minds of thoughtful and experienced adults.

Love of children, observation of human character, and the practice of scientific methods led the Edgeworths to a more promising path. They observed closely the working of the minds of their own children, and noted their attempts to explain the little puzzles of everyday life. Faithful observation and diligent recording had their reward. The Edgeworths got possession of a scientific method—perhaps the first in the annals of education which fairly deserves the name. Unpretending as they were, they laid claim to this merit at least. "To make any progress in the art of education," they say in the preface to their book, "it must be patiently reduced to an experimental science." It was, in truth, a new experimental science which they founded, or rather began to found, for its main principles have, in all probability, yet to be discovered.

There seems to have been something flighty

and exaggerated about Richard Edgeworth. He was a great talker, among other things, and had the sanguine mind of the projector. Byron describes him, in 1821, as "a fine old fellow, of a clarety, elderly, red complexion, but active, brisk, and endless." He became something of a bore in the fashionable world of London during a long visit in 1821; and when a memorial was talked of, pleading for the recall of Mrs. Siddons to the stage, some one suggested a second memorial, for the recall of the Edgeworths to Ireland. There was neither volubility nor self-confidence in Maria Edgeworth, whom everybody liked, and her modesty may have done the book at least as much good as the ingenuity of her father. Every page bears the mark of complete sincerity.

Edgeworth the father had been impressed by Rousseau's writings, and had actually tried the "Education of Nature" upon his eldest son. "I dressed my son without stockings," he says, "with his arms bare, in a jacket and trousers, such as are quite common at present, but which were at that time novel and extraordinary. I succeeded in making him remarkably hardy; I also succeeded in making him fearless of danger, and, what is more difficult, capable of bearing privation of every sort." Thomas Day also, the Day of "Sandford and Merton," advocated

Rousseau's methods, and tried them upon the young women whom he hoped to train as model wives. But the Edgeworths found out before long what was wanting in Rousseau. They began to note down the actual words of real children whose ages are given. The second Mrs. Edgeworth, who started the work, says: "The simple language of childhood has been preserved without alteration," and everything testifies to the fidelity of the report. We have accordingly, in the "Practical Education," none of the unreal sentiment and theatrical effects of "Emile." The Edgeworths were, as they say, "content with nature." The few and simple lessons preserved show the self-restraint practised by those wise teachers. They wished to make the children think, and not to force the thoughts of grown-up people upon them. Nothing was explained to a child that he could possibly find out for himself. The Edgeworths were well aware that "the danger of doing too much in education is greater even than the danger of doing too little." One thing at a time; one new technical term, one little experiment, one distinct idea, is better than "a confused notion of twenty different things." They tell how "a few years ago a gentleman brought two Eskimaux to London: he wished to amuse, and at the same time to astonish, them with the magnificence of the metropolis. For this purpose, after having equipped them like English gentlemen, he took them out one morning to walk through the streets of London. They walked for several hours in silence; they expressed neither pleasure nor admiration at anything which they saw. When their walk was ended, they appeared uncommonly melancholy and stupefied. As soon as they got home, they sat down with their elbows upon their knees, and hid their faces between their hands. The only words they could be brought to utter were, 'too much smoke—too much noise—too much houses—too much men—too much everything.'"

How different is the way of the Edgeworths! "In stating any question to a child, we should avoid letting our own opinion be known, *lest we lead or intimidate his mind.*" See how this precept is carried out in a dialogue which many a reader of "Practical Education" has no doubt silently condemned as useless:—

Father. S—, how many can you take from one?
S— (a boy of five). None.
Father. None! Think; can you take nothing from one?
S—. None, except that one.
Father. Except! Then you can take one from one?
S—. Yes, *that one.*
Father. Very true; but now, can you take two from one?

S—. Yes, if they were figures I could, with a rubber-out. (This child had sums frequently written for him with a black-lead pencil, and he used to rub out his figures when they were wrong with Indian rubber, which he had heard called "rubber-out.")

Father. Yes, you could; but now we will not talk of figures, we will talk of things. There may be one horse or two horses, or one man or two men.

S—. Yes; or one coat or two coats.

Father. Yes; or one thing or two things, no matter what they are. Now could you take two things from one thing?

S—. Yes; if there were three things I could take away two things and leave one.

His father took up a cake from the tea-table.

Father. Could I take two cakes from this one cake?

S—. You could take two pieces.

His father divided the cake into halves, and held up each half so that the child might distinctly see them.

Father. What would you call these two pieces?

S—. Two cakes.

Father. No, not two cakes.

S—. Two biscuits.

Father (holding up a whole biscuit). What is this?

S—. A thing to eat.

Father. Yes, but what would you call it?

S—. A biscuit.

His father broke it into halves, and showed one half.

Father. What would you call this?

S— was silent, and his sister was applied to, who answered, "half a biscuit."

Father. Very well; that's all at present.

This is given to show that the child could not be taught until he grasped his father's train of ideas; but how well it illustrates the patience, not to be broken down, of the teacher, and his readiness to accept any genuine result, however small!

The Edgeworths would have the teacher take advantage of chance openings rather than formally prepare subjects for discussion.

"The king's staghounds," says Mr. White, of Selborne, in his entertaining observations on quadrupeds, "came down to Alton, attended by a huntsman and six yeomen prickers with horns, to try for the stag that has haunted Hartley Wood and its environs for so long a time. Many hundreds of people, horse and foot, attended the dogs to see the deer unharboured; but though the huntsman drew Hartley Wood, and Long-coppice, and Shrub Wood, and Temple-hangers, and in their way back Hartley and Wardleham-hangers, yet no stag could be found. The royal pack, accustomed to have the deer turned out before them, never drew the covers with any address and spirit." Children who are accustomed to have the game started and turned out before them by their preceptors may, perhaps, like the royal pack, lose their wonted address and spirit, and may be disgracefully at a fault in the public chase. Preceptors should not help their pupils out in argument, they should excite them to explain and support their own observations.

Now for another practical example of their method of exciting their pupils to think out problems for themselves.

(January 10th, 1795.) *S*— (eight years old) said that he had been thinking about the wind; and he believed that it was the earth's turning round that made the wind.

M—. Then how comes it that the wind does not blow always the same way?

S—. Aye; that's the thing I can't make out; besides, perhaps the air would stick to the earth as it turns round, as threads stick to my spinning top, and go round with it.

(January 18th, 1796.) *S—* (nine years old). Father, I have thought of a reason for the wind's blowing. When there has been a hot sunshiny day, and when the ground has been wet, the sun attracts a great deal of vapour; then *that* vapour must have room, so it must push away some air to make room for itself; besides, vapour swells with heat, so it must have a *great, great* deal of room, as it grows hotter and hotter; and the moving the air to make way for it must make wind."

We must avoid putting such a meaning upon the words "not to lead or intimidate his mind" as would prohibit regular teaching altogether. But in the history of every intelligent child questions arise which need not be solved at once. They may relate to more advanced parts of the subject in hand, or to subjects not yet taken up. The teacher must be quick to notice when the child's curiosity is roused, and more anxious to urge than to satisfy it. A thinking man has always a number of unsolved questions in his mind, and his intellectual progress depends very much upon the way in which he deals with them. The child may profitably exercise his wits upon them too, and when he is so engaged the teacher will do well to supply the facts called for, to criticise mistaken solutions, but otherwise to meddle as little as possible.

The chapter on Toys is full of sagacity and quiet fun. The best thing I can say to recommend it is that I have seen these suggestions tried with excellent results twice over. A few toys with which children can actually play are worth a houseful of shop toys. Speaking from the practical experience of two generations which came in turn under the influence of the Edgeworths, I recommend trial of the following:—

(1) Wooden bricks, 3 in. by $1\frac{1}{2}$ in. by $\frac{3}{4}$ in. There should be not less than a gross of them; two gross would go into a box 18 in. by 9 in. by 6 in. These bricks will not only make walls, houses, castles, and lighthouses, but railways, regiments, and fleets of ships. The imagination of a child will transform them in a thousand ways. (2) A great heap of sand, say two cartloads. This requires an open space out of doors. (3) Knucklebones of sheep, called in some parts of the country "dibbs." The "dibstones" of Locke are an earthenware substitute. The bone wanted is the *astragalus* (listen to the professor of biology!). There is one in every leg of mutton; but a teacher is absolutely necessary, and I fear that the game is dying out. (4) Toys made by the children themselves. Popguns, skip-jacks, and whistles are easily managed, but here too you must have a teacher.[1]

I find some sensible remarks on rewards and

---

[1] See also "Helplessness and Handiness," p. 22.

punishments. "The fewer the laws we make for children the better." "By diminishing temptations to do wrong, we act more humanely than by multiplying restraints and punishments." In girls' schools, I am told, considerable moral pressure is sometimes exerted to enforce rules of no great importance. Servility and over-conscientiousness are the natural result. Minute regulations are mischievous not only when they are broken, but also when they are kept. "The amiable feelings of the heart," say our authors, "need not be displayed; they may be sufficiently exercised without the stimulus either of our eloquence or our applause. In Madame de Silleri's account of the education of the children of the Duke of Orleans there appears rather too much sentimental artifice and management." The account is too long and too unimportant for quotation at length, but here, as in Rousseau's "Emile," there is clearly "too much sentimental artifice and management." It is evidently Maria Edgeworth who continues:— "Let us be content with nature, or, rather, let us never exchange simplicity for affectation. Nothing hurts young people more than to be watched continually about their feelings, to have their countenances scrutinized, and the degrees of their sensibility measured by the surveying eye of the unmerciful spectator."

"Let us be content with nature" is indeed

the chief lesson to be drawn from "Practical Education." We may as well be content, for we shall get nothing better. The present-day reader, who has perhaps been taught by George Eliot to appreciate complex moral situations and noble sentiments, will be inclined to make light of the simple and old-fashioned morality of the Edgeworths. We require greater subtlety in the delineation of character and a more flexible style than Miss Edgeworth or even Sir Walter Scott commanded. Writers of modern fiction have carried the analysis of imaginary characters to a pitch not dreamt of a hundred years ago, but they have at the same time lowered our interest in fact and reality. The morality of the Edgeworths may be summed up in the words—Love of truth and practice of benevolence. It is not highly wrought fiction nor ingenuity of phrase that can show us anything greater than these.

NATURE-STUDY.[1]

Within my memory there has been a notable improvement in the quality of teachers of all grades. The teacher knows much more than he used to do, and he is more zealous. Perhaps the best teachers of forty years ago were as able as

[1] Part of an Address given to the Teachers' Guild of Great Britain and Ireland, October 13, 1896.

any that now exist; but the average of excellence has risen and is rising. It would be hard to find in a modern school of decent status such teachers as were common when I was a boy—men who did not know their work, and had drifted into teaching because they could find nothing else to do.

But there is nothing perfect, and even the teacher of to-day has his faults. The most serious fault that I find in him is that he is an extinguisher of curiosity. It is not the schoolmaster only; the professor is as bad or worse. All of us deaden curiosity by telling our pupils or students a great deal that they do not want to know. This is fatal to the habit of inquiring into the things around us, which I would like to see in every intelligent person. Most of us are born with this turn of mind, but it is drilled out of us by parents and nursemaids and teachers, who all say: "Don't bother with your foolish questions, but listen to me!" Curiosity is gradually stifled under lists of capes and rivers, lists of kings and queens, lists of compounds of chlorine and oxygen, lists of "metals, semi-metals, and distinguished philosophers." "Mangnall's Questions," under which the children of England groaned for forty years, is, I hope, extinct, but books not very much better are still in use in school and college. Our practical conception of teaching is still that of presenting to the learner's mind assorted packets of information. We tell them much, trusting that some small percentage may stick in the memory. The thirst for knowledge, the habit of inquiry, we do not teach.

I speak with confidence on this deadening of curiosity, because of long experience. I usually offer to my class as their first lesson in biology the common frog. I often begin with the skin of the frog first, as the most accessible part. The class examine the skin, and then we see what they have found out about it. We want a term of comparison, and I naturally take the human skin. What has their daily and hourly observation of the human skin during seventeen or eighteen years taught them? So little that the few answers to my questions are almost always drawn from Huxley's "Physiology."

It is the same for some time afterwards. I want to make my students inquirers; but their chief anxiety is to know what they are to read. They can learn from text-books, or diagrams, or lectures; but to learn from Nature, by the help of their five senses, is a thing that they are disinclined to try further, as if they had found out (what is very likely true) that Nature is not so helpful in passing examinations as what certain people have said about Nature. They must be told what to look for before they will open their eyes; they must be told what to think, or they will not think at all. The true aim of the teacher is to excite and ennoble the curiosity, but we too often teach so as to quench it for ever.

Almost any text-book will show that we begin to teach science at the wrong end. The student, new to all the properties of light, is taught after this fashion: "The light of the sun and other celestial bodies, of the electric spark, and of all ordinary flames, is of a compound nature, consisting of differently refrangible rays. The violet rays are the most refrangible, and the red rays the least." It may be years afterwards that he sees some lecture experiment which gives for the first time a real meaning to these words. Meanwhile the inquiry—the opportunity of fixing the beginner's mind upon the natural problem—has been flung away as useless.

How then would the enlightened teacher go to work? Turn to Edgeworth's "Practical Education" and you will see. A boy of nine finds a kind of rainbow on the floor. He calls his sister to see, and wonders how it came there. The sun shines bright through the window. The boy moves several things upon which the light falls, saying: "This is not it. Nor this." At last, when he moves a tumbler of water, the rainbow vanishes. There are some violets in the tumbler, which he thinks may explain the colours on the floor. But when the violets are removed the colours remain.

Then he thinks it may be the water. He empties the glass. The colours remain, but they are fainter. This leads him to suppose that the water and the glass together make the rainbow. "But," he adds, "there is no glass in the sky, yet there is a rainbow, so that I think the water alone would do, if we could but hold it together without the glass." He then pours the water slowly out of the tumbler into a basin, which he places in the sunlight, and sees the colours on the floor twinkling behind the water as it falls.

All this is admirable. We see that the boy had been trained to observe, and to think, and to inquire. His elders were careful not to tell him what he could find out for himself; they were content to leave the inquiry unfinished, waiting for a good opportunity to return to it. No sequel is given, but it is easy to see how the lesson might be followed up. Suppose that one day a triangular glass prism—let us say, one of the drops of a crystal chandelier—is procured. We put such a prism into the boy's hand, and let him occupy himself for five minutes with looking through it. He will first discover that he can see nothing which is immediately behind the prism. Then he will observe that, as the prism is turned about, two kinds of pictures of neighbouring objects are formed, the one set undistorted and like the reflections in a mirror, the other set distorted and curiously coloured. Look at a strip of white paper through the prism, so as to get the coloured fringes. On the left side of the strip the colours are red and yellow; on the right they are green, blue, and violet. But if we look at a black object through the prism, we find that the red and yellow lie to the right, the green, blue, and violet to the left. Let the boy observe these things and try to account for them. It will help him if he remarks that when we are looking at white paper on a dark ground we have the white inside the black. If we reverse the case, and put the black inside the white, we may expect the coloured fringes to be reversed. Let him look at narrow and wide strips of paper through his prism. Experiment and suggestion will enable him gradually to discover the secret of the fringes.

Then we can employ a prism to throw a spectrum upon the wall. I think I should show a good spectrum first of all, to make it clear what is the effect to be produced. But before the apparatus had been minutely examined I should derange it. The boy, or the class of boys, must be taught where the adjustable slit and the lens can be most advantageously placed, and why; and how the prism is to be set. They must also, each for himself, set up the whole thing, so as to produce a good result. Until they have done this more than once they have not learnt the lesson for good.

Thus instead of a dead piece of information, received passively from without, we get a lesson in the interrogation of Nature. We learn what we are at the time eager to know. We feel a real difficulty, and are then shown how that difficulty has been overcome by more powerful minds. We learn by doing, and get no result that we have not worked for.

The spirit of inquiry is only to be communicated by those who have it, who habitually inquire themselves. This amounts to saying that no one ought to teach science who is not in his way an original thinker upon science. Are we then to demand that every teacher of elementary science is to be fit to carry on original research? That word is far too imposing, but I hold that in some measure, however modest, the teacher must be an investigator. He must put and answer questions daily, not out of books or by appealing to other people, but by his own observations and experiments. The results may be too unimportant or too familiar for publication, but the habit is essential to the life of the teaching.

When we look around for likely subjects for lessons in the art of inquiry, we shall find them few or many according to our power of seeing them. They lie about us in incredible numbers, and the only difficulty is to discover the possibilities of each. The things which in general answer best are those which are ready to hand, those about which the curiosity of the learners is already excited, and those which open out really important questions. All these conditions are satisfied by the living things, plants or animals, which surround us everywhere. The study of living things is a study of exquisite mechanisms, illustrating the most intricate and abstruse, as well as the simplest, scientific principles. We can never exhaust their complexity, and yet, beautiful and elaborate as they are, they are to be had in extravagant profusion. We pull them to pieces without scruple; they are perpetually ready for observation and experiment.

Here then is a great educational opportunity, and our problem is how to handle it so as to secure a lasting good for our pupils. It is dreadfully easy to misuse the opportunity. We perhaps say: "The naturalist has a technical language of his own; I will teach you that language." Or we say: "Natural history is nothing if it is not systematic; let us work through the systems of the zoologist and botanist." Alas! the interest, on which all else depends, does not survive such handling as this. Learned language, lists, fine-drawn distinctions, dried specimens, these are at best the accessories of natural history, accessories which hinder instead of helping, unless they are made to serve a living intelligence.

Everything falls into its right place as soon as we focus our minds upon the thing which really signifies—that is, upon life. Of all things which can occupy the living man, there is none quite so interesting as that mysterious gift of life which we share with so many other creatures. The child, and every grown person of unsophisticated tastes, is eager to know about living things, how they manage, what difficulties and hardships they have to face, what expedients they employ. Especially if the observation of lower forms throws any side light upon human life, we are all attention. As much detail as you please, provided that it helps to solve some problem of the living world; but let us offer no unintelligible details to young minds, at least.

So little have naturalists looked upon plants and animals as living things that almost every subject is new. In selecting a subject for study, I have been in the habit of looking out for some very common thing, which I can see almost whenever I please. I find my best subjects in my own garden, or in the next field, or in the brook at the bottom of the valley. All are common, but hardly any have been worked out beforehand. I give this advice to my juniors:

Take the things which lie close about you, and study *them*. Study them as living things, and never fear but that you will find plenty in them that is new.

Study the things alive, and do not omit to examine carefully the spot where they grow. When you carry them away, remember that you may be leaving half the story behind you. How can you understand the adaptation of the organism to its surroundings, if the surroundings are unobserved or forgotten?

Draw much. Drawing is often the best way of studying, and the best way of taking notes. Do not make rough drawings, but draw to scale, and with so much care that you can always rely upon any drawing that you find in your notebook. I am accustomed to prepare the drawings for a memoir first. While they are in hand I get the facts of structure right, and have time to consider how they can be interpreted. To write the memoir, when all this has been done, is an easy matter.

When you describe, use the plainest and least technical words that you can find. It will save you from mistaking your own meaning, as learned writers continually do, and will conciliate your readers, if you write for others.

Try to make yourself an habitual questioner of Nature. You must incessantly ask: Why is this so? When you are working without a question in your head, you are probably working to little purpose. I would not have you do much of what is called *collecting materials*. Natural history in our day is being choked by unassimilated facts. We want every worker to think upon what he does. Do not be discouraged if you cannot at first put likely questions, or if you cannot answer the questions which you put. Robinson Crusoe swam twice round the ship before he could get aboard, and then saw a rope hanging down which he wondered not to have spied before. I must warn you that for a long time your answers to your own questions are pretty sure to be wrong. You get at the right answers by continually rejecting those that are wrong or incomplete. Be strict as Rhadamanthus with your own explanations; you cannot criticise them too sharply.

I must not forget that you are a Teachers' Guild. Many of you are working teachers, and you will expect me to say something about the study of Nature under school conditions. How can we teach children, twenty or thirty at a time, to study Nature with profit?

The good teacher will have a quick eye for opportunities. A wheelbarrow will illustrate certain mechanical principles admirably, and we all know what a capital lesson can be founded upon a candle-flame. A potato seems to me a first-rate choice for an object-lesson. We all know something about it, and are all glad to know more. Yet how little the average town child knows about the growth of the potato! I venture to say that many of the poorer children in towns are not aware that the potatoes which we see at table grow upon a plant. I know how glad they are to see the great tangled mass of roots of a potato plant, dug fresh from the soil, with the tubers, great and small, clinging to them, and to learn what the "eyes" of the potato really are.

The good teacher will be careful to observe that golden rule: Never to tell the children anything which they can find out for themselves. The information gained is at best a small matter, and we must not sacrifice for the sake of information the habit of inquiry, which is infinitely more important. You want to make the children observant, inquisitive, and at length thoughtful; you do not want to make them encyclopædias of information.

We must diligently practise the great maxim: "Learn by doing." Every lesson should suggest something to be collected, or something to be drawn, or something to be made. At first we may well be satisfied with very simple and easy practical exercises, but let us not be satisfied to go on with such things too long. I have often been disappointed to see big boys and girls whose only natural-history occupation was pasting dried plants into books or setting butterflies. After years of natural-history work, they ought to be more enterprising than that, if they have been well taught. I would have them aspire to making good experiments, or doing some other thing which is not mechanical.

When we are teaching boys we must remember what boys are like. They are often acute and eager, but they tire of long-continued effort. You can interest them in your questions; you can make them work for you, especially with hand and eye; but do not expect to get continuous and systematic work out of them. That can only be got by injurious pressure. Their strength is not yet mature. But there comes a time when the restless and easily fatigued boy has by time and gentle exercise become capable of prolonged exertion, able to think severely and continuously. Then is the time to aspire to mastery of great subjects, and to learn what the command of powerful deductive methods means. We begin with short trials; we hope to end, in some cases at least, with comprehensive and well-ordered knowledge. At first it is enough to stimulate the curiosity; in a later stage we must seek to ennoble it. We want to turn the short-lived curiosity of the child, which is but a fire of straw, into a better and more lasting thing—I mean the love of knowledge. But all this belongs to a later stage. I only mention it here lest it should be supposed that I would teach all science by means of object-lessons.

We are to begin slowly, as we teach a child to walk. Help, but not too much help, is wanted. We are to encourage, to watch, and unobtrusively to guide, these early efforts. Patience in this stage will save much trouble in the end, and perhaps the worst fault that we can commit is to be in a hurry to see results. But as the pupil grows stronger, we hope to see him do more and more for himself. The time will come when the slightest hint will suffice.

We shall help to ennoble the curiosity if we give the student some faint sense of the immensity and complexity of Nature, and some notion, however inadequate, of what has been accomplished by the long efforts of mankind. It is enough for the boy of nine to find out that sunlight passing through a tumbler of water may form rainbow colours on the table-cloth, but the young fellow of twenty-two should be acquainted with the growth of optics under the hands of Descartes and Huygens and Newton and Young and Fresnel and Hertz. In the same way the later lessons in natural history should be seasoned with biography. Even children will be glad to hear how Swammerdam and Leeuwenhoeck worked, and what kind of microscopes they used. Make a Leeuwenhoeck microscope for them, and let them look through it. Réaumur is a storehouse of natural history, which the well-informed teacher will gladly draw from. When he does so, let him tell the story of Réaumur's life. When you bring out one of Darwin's discoveries, as you often will, do not omit to speak of his perseverance and his candour, and his long fight with bigotry. After all, it is the human side of a great discovery which has most permanent interest. The greatest thing on earth is man; the greatest thing in man is mind.

You will, no doubt, be ready to tell me of the difficulty of doing all that I want done, and I will admit beforehand that the difficulties are many. The first and to many teachers the most pressing difficulty of all is that of time. It costs much time and effort to get up really good lessons. How shall a teacher who is already giving, say, six or eight hours a day to the routine work of school, make elaborate preparation for a single lesson? I reply that I would have the hours given to teaching reduced, so as to be compatible with thorough preparation.

Secondly, I would have helps provided. For example, once a week I meet a number of teachers, and go over with them the matter of an object-lesson. Then they all spend two hours in making apparatus, or in preparation of some kind for the school-lesson. That is another and legitimate way of saving time. But if both these expedients are impracticable in a particular case, I still would not give up the true method. I should say: If the time at command allows only one lesson a year to be prepared with due thoroughness, prepare and give that one lesson. I should count upon the strong probability that the good lessons will in time drive out the bad ones. Even to have given a single good lesson is some security against hasty slipshod lessons, without thought or method.

If you give lessons of the right sort, your pupils will grow observant of the things about them. It is a pleasure to see the children posing one another with questions about every unfamiliar object. For instance, I have overheard them asking among themselves, What is the use of the oval board which often hangs by two holes outside a railway signal box? If you have never put such a question, if you do not know of the existence of such boards, depend upon it your curiosity is insufficiently trained.

You will have your reward if your pupils,

whatever may be their occupations in after life, turn out handy, inquisitive, thoughtful, accurate, and sympathetic towards all the nobler forms of human effort. To train such men and women, and not to train botanists or zoologists, is the real aim of the study of Nature.

REMARKS ON TWO PASSAGES IN BAIN'S "EDUCATION AS A SCIENCE."

The leading idea of the book is arrangement of the teacher's thoughts and more accurate definition of the terms used in teaching. But there are many practical discussions on methods, and a very important estimate of the value of Latin and Greek as school subjects. I am not in the least competent to criticise the more abstract parts of the book, and will merely offer some remarks on two isolated passages.

These observations will serve to illustrate the working of the emotion named Curiosity, which is justly held to be a great power in teaching. Curiosity expresses the emotions of knowledge viewed as desire; and, more especially, the desire to surmount an intellectual difficulty once felt. Genuine curiosity belongs to the stage of advanced and correct views of the world.

Much of the curiosity of children, and of others besides children, is a spurious article. Frequently it is a mere display of egotism, the delight in giving trouble, in being pandered to and served. Questions are put, not from the desire of rational information, but from the love of excitement. Occasionally, the inquisitiveness of a child provides an opportunity for imparting a piece of real information, but far oftener not. By ingeniously circumventing a scientific fact, one not too high for a child's comprehension, we may awaken curiosity, and succeed in impressing the fact. Try a child to lift a heavy weight first by the direct pull, and then by a lever or a set of pulleys, and probably you will excite some surprise and wonder, with a desire to know something further about the instrumentality. But one fatal defect of the childish mind is the ascendency of the personal or anthropomorphic conception of cause. This, no doubt, is favourable to the theological explanation of the world, but wholly unsuited to physical science. A child, if it had any curiosity at all, would like to know what makes the grass grow, the rain fall, the wind howl, and generally all things that are occasional and exceptional, an indifference being contracted towards what is familiar, constant, and regular. When anything goes wrong, the child has the wish to set it right, and is anxious to know what will answer the purpose : this is the inlet of practice, and, by this, correct knowledge may find its way to the mind, provided the power of comprehension is sufficiently matured. Still, the radical obstacle remains—the impossibility of approaching science at random, or taking it in any order; we must begin at the proper beginning, and we may not always contrive to tickle the curiosity at the exact stage of the pupil's understanding. Every teacher knows, or should know, the little arts of giving a touch of wonder and mystery to a fact before giving the explanation, all which is found to tell in the regular march of exposition, but would be lost labour in any other course.

The very young, those that we are working upon by

gentle allurement, are not fully competent to learn the "how" or the "wherefore" of any important natural fact; they cannot even be made to desire the thing in the proper way. They are open chiefly to the charm of sense, novelty, and variety, which, together with accidental charm or liking, impresses the pictorial or concrete aspects of the world, whether quiescent or changing, the last being the most powerful. They further are capable of understanding the more palpable conditions of many changes without penetrating to ultimate causes. They learn that to light a fire there must be fuel and a light applied; that the growth of vegetables needs planting or sowing, together with rain and sunshine through a summer season. The empirical knowledge of the world that preceded science is still the knowledge that the child passes through in the way to science; and all this may be guided so as to prepare for the future scientific revelations. In other respects, the so-called curiosity of children is chiefly valuable as yielding ludicrous situations for our comic literature.

All this conflicts seriously with my own experience. I have learned to count upon the inquisitiveness of children. Not only is it, as I have fancied, the great instrument of the teacher, but I have come to believe that it can nearly always be roused or created. When I fail to rouse curiosity I blame my own awkwardness, or else inquire whether the children are not by nature or education unusually stupid. Whatever may be the cause, if curiosity cannot be roused, my teaching is paralyzed. It will be understood that I am speaking of teaching in its more characteristic forms.

No doubt, practice in sums and other mechanical, though necessary, pieces of schoolwork can go on in the absence of any stimulus to curiosity. But every step in reasoning, every distinct accession of knowledge, seems to come most naturally by means of questions. "Why is this? What result shall we get if we try that? How do we know that something else is a fact?" And the questions are not to be dry and formal, not mere tests of the attention and memory: they should be in great part aimed at points which have not yet been mastered by the pupil—exploratory rather than recapitulatory questions, though both are useful. The questions need to be piquant; the habit of questioning wants to be firmly established. I remember a visitor who dropped in to dine at our family table, and said afterwards: "I never took a meal so seasoned with questions in my whole life." Not only does the teacher or parent who is bent upon making children think become an inveterate questioner, but the children themselves take it up. They persecute their relatives and friends: what is more to the point, they get a fixed habit of questioning *things*, of trying experiments. I know of no habit of mind which can be more surely set up in fairly sensible children of six and upwards than that of curiosity about the things around them. The curiosity, though artificially aroused, is real enough, and productive. Many a bit of information which I value has been brought to me by young people whom I had taught to be inquisitive.

The practical difference between teaching those who want to know and those who don't want to know is as great as can be imagined. Let the teacher "begin at the proper beginning," and prosecute his "regular march of exposition" without much reference to the curiosity of the child, and he may make a learned man, but he will neither make nor help to make an investigator. This is probably one reason why men who have shown a genius for research have so often in youth rebelled against their teachers. To be taught what you have no curiosity about is very nearly the same thing as to be bored, and impatience of boredom is a wholesome feature, which often shows itself early in original minds.

Perhaps I may be told that the experience of the family is not valuable in school, where so many different children have to be trained together. But I am speaking from experience in the classroom and the public lecture, as well as in the family. Whether you have two, or forty, or a thousand people to teach, you must open the way by exciting their curiosity. It can be done, and there is, I firmly believe, no good way of doing without it.

I am pulled up again by what I read on page 95:—

Unreasoning blind faith is indispensable in beginning any art or science; the pupil has to lay up a stock of notions before having any materials for discovery or origination. There is a right moment for relaxing this attitude, and for assuming the exercise of independence; but it has scarcely arrived while the schoolmaster is still at work. Even in the higher walks of University teaching, independence is premature, unless in some exceptional minds, and the attempt of masters to proceed upon it, and to invite the free criticism of pupils, does not appear to have been very fruitful.

Author's Note.—It would lead us too far, although it might not be uninstructive, to reflect upon the evil side of this fondness for giving a new and self-suggested cast to all received knowledge. It introduces change for the mere sake of change, and never lets well alone. It multiplies variations of form and phraseology for expressing the same facts, and so renders all subjects more perplexed than they need be; not to speak of controverting what is established, because it is established, and allowing nothing ever to settle. Owing to a dread of the feverish love of change, certain works that have accidentally received an ascendancy, such as the Elements of Euclid, are retained notwithstanding their imperfections. The acquiescent multitude of minds regard this as a less evil than letting loose the men of action and revolution to vie with each other in distracting alterations, while there is no judicial power to hold the balance. It is a received maxim in the tactics of legislation that no scheme, however well matured, can pass a popular body without amendment; it is not in collective human nature to accept anything *simpliciter*, without having a finger in the pie.

I am not so thorough-going a rationalist that I would argue with the child about his multiplication table, but I should try to shake his "unreasoning blind faith" long before he left school. Euclid is perfectly fair game for the doubter. A boy who has the misfortune to learn his geometry from Euclid should be encouraged to pick out his author's silent assumptions, and at a later stage to criticise his cumbrous methods. When we begin to teach biology to a young fellow we wage war upon "unreasoning blind faith." He is from the first bid to form his notions upon what he sees, not upon what he is told to look for. Nothing promises better for the young student than a propensity to check every statement that is not self-evident.

There is at least one eminent man of science on Professor Bain's side. The late Mr. Todhunter, in his "Conflict of Studies," gives his opinion in these terms:—

To take another example. We assert that, if the resistance of the air be withdrawn, a sovereign and a feather will fall through equal spaces in equal times. Very great credit is due to the person who first imagined the well-known experiment to illustrate this, but it is not obvious what is the special benefit now gained by seeing a lecturer repeat the process. It may be said that a boy takes more interest in the matter by seeing for himself, or by performing for himself, that is, by working the handle of the air-pump. This we admit, while we continue to doubt the educational value of the transaction. The boy would also probably take much more interest in football than in Latin grammar; but the measure of his interest is not identical with that of the importance of the subjects. It may be said that the fact makes a stronger impression on the boy through the medium of his sight—that he believes it more confidently. I say that this ought not to be the case. If he does not believe the statements of his tutor—probably a clergyman of mature knowledge, recognized ability, and blameless character—his suspicion is irrational, and manifests a want of the power of appreciating evidence, a want fatal to his success in that branch of science which he is supposed to be cultivating.

I am glad to be able to set against this opinion the practice of another eminent man of science.

"He [Professor H. N. Moseley] had somehow developed in early youth the most deep-rooted scepticism which I ever came across among men of my own age; hence it was the reality of the work which he did in the dissecting-room at the museum which delighted him and gave him confidence that there was "something in it" worthy of his intellectual effort. With unfeigned astonishment he would say, on dissecting out the nervous system of the mollusk or some such structure, "It is like the picture, after all!" He had a profound disbelief in the statements made in books unless he could verify them for himself, and it was this habit of mind, perceived and encouraged by Rolleston, which made him in after life so admirable an observer and so successful as a discoverer of new facts. Rolleston used to say that you had only to put down Moseley on a hill-side with a piece of string and an old nail, and in an hour or two he would have discovered some natural object of surpassing interest.[1]

[1] Professor Ray Lankester in *Nature*, November 26, 1891.

I cannot define any stage in scientific study where scepticism is not laudable. The authority of the teacher should only extend to such externals as the order in which the work is to be taken, and the arbitrary names which are to be given to things. I should shrink from saying to any one: "You are to believe this statement of fact," however sure I felt of the fact. In all scientific work the spirit of inquiry and scepticism is so indispensable that we should be slow to quench it, even when it becomes troublesome.

Do I perhaps offend some readers by speaking of scepticism as a thing honourable and necessary? We hear it denounced as destructive simply. But there is scepticism and scepticism. We know the scepticism which says: "There is nothing new and nothing true, and it doesn't matter," and we also know the "active scepticism" of which Goethe speaks, bent upon conquering itself.[1] Active scepticism, the longing for reality, and for the closest contact with the facts of the case, will look upon the testimony of the blameless clergyman as a poor thing in comparison. Fact is not only better than all imaginable fictions—it is better than the truest description. Hence it is noticeable, and perhaps surprising to some readers, to find Moseley's scepticism spoken of as

[1] Some readers will be reminded of what Huxley says about this (Essay on Descartes' Discourse).

productive. He would not take things on trust, and so he came to see wonders on every hill-side.

FROEBEL AND PESTALOZZI.

I made real acquaintance with Froebel very late in my career as a teacher. For a long time he was to me nothing more than the author of the kindergarten system. When I heard him quoted, it was with what I considered exaggerated respect, as a master whose very words were binding. I looked into the "Menschenerziehung," and lost my way. For I found there questionable principles enunciated as self-evident; at other times I found Froebel solemnly asserting propositions so abstract that they had lost all body, like gases at a pressure of a thousandth of an atmosphere, and yet he plainly expected you to receive these propositions, notwithstanding their tenuity, as mental food. I found little trace of the process by which his conclusions had been attained; only at long intervals some hint of the author's own history and of his own observations. His reflections and even his practical instructions were mixed up with philosophy and poetry. The philosophy I did not accept, and the poetry I did not feel.

My eyes were at length opened by W. H. Herford's "Student's Froebel." Here I got the best of our author's "Education of Man" in clear English, the more obscure passages being excised or condensed into single sentences, and the truly significant rightly emphasized. I now read Froebel for the first time with real profit, and began to see what he had to teach me. I have read and re-read him in this completely practicable form, and have found it possible to carry some of his maxims into practice, although the time in which I had young children about me every day has unfortunately slipped by.

How can I help to bring Froebel to the notice of other teachers? Herford's "Froebel" is the real door of access for English men and women; but, as people do not all or at once go to the authors whom we cite, I will here take up a few of the passages which have been most profitable to myself. Like almost all writers of his class, Froebel is the better for selection and abridgment.

> A child who seems good *outwardly* is often not good *inwardly*, i.e., does not try to be good out of love and with self-control, but is contented to seem so; while one who is outwardly rough and wilful often has within it a most zealous endeavour to do right. An apparently inattentive child may have within it a steady thoughtfulness that hinders its heeding things outward. Therefore education and instruction should from the very first be passive, observant, protective, rather than prescribing, determining, interfering. (Page 5.)[1]

[1] The references are to the "Student's Froebel," Part I.

The word "passive" may present some difficulty. I can imagine an experienced teacher saying: "Does Froebel require us to stay our hand altogether, and cease to guide the lessons? No doubt the guiding hand must be little seen. It is better to suggest than to command; better for the child to suggest than merely to respond to suggestion. But, if the teacher really *lets go*, surely the lessons will become chaotic." Our imaginary objector is thinking chiefly about *instruction*, whereas Froebel is discussing *training*—the development of the child's mind. Throughout the whole discussion he is thinking of the conditions under which a living organism can be developed. Now, the mind cannot be shaped or consciously made: it must grow. We sometimes talk about "forming the mind" of a child. We could as soon form a flower or a bird. Nature will form the child's mind for us if we will only give her fair play and be satisfied with supplying the right external conditions. In artificial fowl-hatching we supply the eggs with fresh air, moisture, and a carefully-regulated temperature. We are particular to turn and cool the eggs every day, having learnt to do so from the brooding hen. Later on, when the chick has escaped from the egg, we give it food, the same in kind and quantity as nature prescribes. All the rest we leave to those unknown forces which direct the transformation of crude products into a complex living thing. In training a child it is equally necessary to observe and follow nature. When we give information, which in some degree answers to the food of the mind, let us give it in no larger doses than the intellectual appetite (which we also know by the name of "curiosity") can deal with. When we offer stimuli, let us make sure that they exhilarate, and do not depress. Let us incessantly watch the result of our treatment, like an experimenter who tries with hesitation and on a small scale what he will afterwards try boldly on a large scale. And let us be careful to provide the growing mind with those three most necessary conditions which appear next in Froebel's exposition—*space and time and rest.*

To young plants and animals we give space and time and rest, knowing that they will unfold to beauty by laws working in each. We avoid acting on them by force, for we know that such intrusion upon their natural growth could only injure their development. Yet man treats the young human being as if it were a piece of wax, a lump of clay, out of which he can mould what he will. (Page 5.)

Observe the change since the humane and reasonable Locke could speak of the young mind as "white paper or wax, to be moulded and fashioned as one pleases."

"Space and time and rest." Let these words

sink into our minds. How little are they to be reconciled with the everyday tasks of many a teacher—the rapid preparation of an immature youth for technical business, or the hot-house forcing of the promising schoolboy into a winner of scholarships! We make so much of machinery! Sagacious and public-spirited men eagerly discuss the organization of secondary education, and believe that they are doing good service to the State. I believe that they are, but I should like to whisper in their ears: "Development—space and time and rest."

In good education, genuine instruction, and true teaching, necessity calls forth freedom, law evokes self-determination, external constraint calls forth internal free will, hate from without evokes love from within. Wherever hatred begets hatred, and law calls into being deceit and crime; wherever constraint produces slavish feeling, and necessity sense of bondage; wherever pressure destroys inward activity, and severity engenders depression and falsehood, there all genuine education, all true working of teaching and instruction, is at an end. That this latter state of things may be escaped and the former attained, whoever acts with authority must go to work observantly. This is secured when all education, teaching, instruction, though acting with authority, bears yet the incontestable stamp of being itself subject to an overruling law, an inevitable necessity, which excludes caprice. All true education and teaching, therefore every genuine educator and teacher, has to be always, in every detail, two-sided: to give and take, join and divide, command and obey, act and suffer, manage and let alone, be fixed and movable. The child and pupil is to be so likewise, and between the two—tutor and pupil, command and obedience—rules unseen a third term, whereto tutor and pupil are alike and equally subject. This third is the *ideal best*, the *abstract right*, as it issues from the conditions of each case and expresses itself impersonally. The teacher has to express simply and firmly, sometimes even gravely and severely, his clear acquaintance with and quiet obedience to this third term. The pupil, too, has a wonderfully fine feeling for it. A child rarely fails to see whether what parent and teacher order or forbid comes from themselves personally, arbitrarily, or is the expression of universal and necessary truth speaking through them. (Page 8.)

The whole of the last paragraph is summed up in the word *reasonableness*, but Froebel's lengthy statement of the case is impressive. What is meant by "hate from without evoking love from within"? I suppose that this is taken from the Christian teaching: "Love your enemies; bless them that curse you." If we are not equal to this, we may try to carry out the maxim of Marcus Aurelius: "Let the wrong done to you stop there [and not bring forth more wrong]." The imperious and self-willed teacher stands condemned from of old. "For I advise their parents and governors always to carry this in their minds," says John Locke, "that children are to be treated as *rational* creatures."

The danger with the untrained teacher of our

own days is not so much that he should be harsh and tyrannical, as that he should venerate his science or his language too much. Latin, chemistry, and the rest belong to the service of man, and are in themselves nothing. Let us not sacrifice our pupils because we cannot bear the Latin composition or algebra which we teach to be less than complete. "Non l'objet, le savoir, mais le sujet, c'est l'homme."[1]

Parents should consider their child in relation to all its stages of development, without overlooking any. If, especially, they would consider that the vigorous and complete unfolding and improvement of each succeeding stage of life depend on the vigorous, complete, and original development of every preceding stage. This point is too often overlooked or unheeded by parents. They assume the human being to be a boy if he has assumed boy-age; they assume the human being to be a youth and man because he has reached man's years. But the boy is not a boy, nor the youth a youth, simply because he has attained the age of boy and youth, but by virtue of having lived through first child- and then boy-hood, faithful to the claims of his soul and mind and body. Just so man becomes a man, not simply by reaching the average years of manhood, but by fulfilling the duties of all preceding stages of life—childhood, boyhood, youth. Parents, otherwise able and intelligent, will require a child to show itself already a boy or youth; especially ask the boy to show himself a man; thus skipping the stages of boy and youth. It is one

---

[1] Michelet; quoted from Quick's edition of Locke "On Education."

thing to see and heed in the child or boy—in germ or outline—the youth or man that will one day be; it is quite another to look upon and behave to the actual boy as though he were already a man; to expect child and boy to show himself youth and man; to feel and think, act and behave, as though he really were so. Parents who expect this overlook or have forgotten the processes through which alone they themselves have become able parents and useful human beings; for this was by living through the very stages of life which they now wish their child to skip. (Page 17.)

Every child, and later every boy or youth, of what rank or condition soever, should spend an hour or two daily in productive work. (Page 21.)

This very useful advice may be realized in various ways: gardening, carpentry, the home arts, and the Slöjd of our generation are likely things to try. In my own household we have encouraged the children to set the table, and occasionally to get ready the lighter meals. Care must be taken that the productive work does not become monotonous or in any way irksome. It should not be the task of a servant, but the pleasure of the willing. The rule of *an hour or two daily* need not, in well-to-do families, be observed at all strictly. But the habit of helping is invaluable; it makes the children handy, cheerful, and obliging.

Play is the highest point of human development in the child-stage. (Page 30.)

The highest, because it is the free expression

of the chief faculties of the child. It exercises limbs, heart and lungs, senses, ingenuity, memory, judgment, temper, and social gifts. We must be watchful even with the games of young children: they have so little discretion, and are often eager beyond their powers. I have known a boy of nine make himself ill by spinning his top too long and too furiously. Even the gentle exercises of the kindergarten quickly overtax the strength of certain children. Observation, without restraint, is all that is wanted in most cases.

Thus a true mother gently follows up the life that is springing everywhere in her child, strengthens it, and thus wakens and unfolds more and more the wider life that still slumbers within it. The rest [formal, artificial child-trainers] assume a vacuum in the child, and try to put life into it, make the child as empty as they believe it to be, and give it death. (Page 37.)

Vacuum, *tabula rasa*, white paper, and all the other metaphors borrowed from inorganic or manufactured objects, are thoroughly untrue. They leave out the essential fact, viz., that the child is capable of natural development and incapable of any other. It is by no means our main duty to "impart knowledge." Knowledge pumped or stuffed in will be a mere dead load. What the child profits by is the carefully considered opportunity, the right hint, the right question, the right fact supplied at the right time—that is, when the child is glad to get hold of it. We can help Nature, it is true; but it is more by observing and protecting than by prescribing and interfering. Let us give to our children the space and time and rest that we give to young plants and animals. Our present crude and ignorant methods are like cramming useful things (loaves, turnips, nails, stockings) into a great sack, so that we may take them out as we want them. But Epictetus long ago pointed out the fallacy. "The sheep," says he, "are not to produce the grass which they have eaten, but wool and milk."[1]

The child has a deep and true feeling of what it may gain and learn from you, if you will let it. That is why it keeps near you, wherever you are, whatever you are doing. Do not send it away ungently, do not drive it from you; be not impatient of its questions, its continual questioning: with every cross repelling word you destroy a bud, a shoot of its life-tree. But do not answer in words, where it can answer itself without your word. As soon as, and as far as, they have strength and experience, give them the conditions of the question, and let them make out the answer from their own knowledge. (Page 44.)

[1] "Enchiridion," xlvi. These words, quoted by Lord Playfair at the inauguration of the Yorkshire College, made a great impression on me at a time when I was far from a right understanding of the function of the teacher.

Thus the Edgeworths bid us not to lead or intimidate the child's mind, and Pestalozzi commands us: "Never, if we can help it, to deprive children of the *sacred right of Discovery*."

I cannot find room for all that the teacher should study. "Boyish Faults" ("Student's Froebel," page 61) is full of wisdom, but too long for quotation.

Do not say, country schoolmaster, "I know nothing of natural objects: I do not even know their names." By faithful observation of nature you can acquire for yourself, however humble has been your education, far higher and more thorough outward and inward knowledge, more vivid acquaintance with the particular and the manifold than any books at all within your means could teach you. Moreover the so-called higher knowledge usually rests on phenomena and perceptions which the simplest person is able to make; aye, on observations which, if we have but eyes to see, we can make with little or no expense more beautifully than by the most costly experiment. The country teacher must bring himself to this by persevering observation; he must specially let himself be led to it by the world of youth, by the boys he has about him. (Page 81.)

So true, so simple, and yet to the majority so impossible!

Alas, that the commonplace should be so unintelligible, and the self-evident prove so hard to comprehend! How comes it to pass that proof should be needed, or even reiterated assertion, that in botany, for instance, it is the seed I have myself dissected, seen open and grow, that becomes mine—not the definitions, however clear, of chlorophyll and cotyledon; that in chemistry the acid wherewith I often stained my clothes, the phosphorus that once burned my fingers, have impressed on my memory indelible traces, while manuals and primers have left scarce a wrack behind?[1]

There is much more in this book which the teacher who would understand his art should make his very own. The great maxim "Learn by doing" is not to be found here, though it already existed, as yet unformulated, in Froebel's mind. Thorough conviction of the value of Froebel's methods is to be got in one way only, and that is by practising them.

I like to close these notes with words of gratitude to Froebel, who has helped me greatly in my own teaching. But Froebel was not the first to show the path. The best of what he knew he learnt from Pestalozzi. It was a Pestalozzian, Gruner, who made Froebel a teacher, and Froebel worked for two years under Pestalozzi himself, at Yverdun.

Pestalozzi, who suggested many of the Froebelian methods, and whose gentle temper shows itself in many a Froebelian saying, had also been touched by an impulse from without. In his early days, when a Zürich student, he had read Rousseau's "Emile" attentively; indeed he tried Rousseau's methods upon his own son.

[1] W. H. Herford, *The School*, p. 19.

Not only Froebel and Pestalozzi, but Basedow, the Edgeworths, and who can say how many other educational reformers, drew inspiration from Rousseau. It was he who proclaimed in a voice that sounded over all Europe, that we must return to Nature, that the real things of life concern us more than all the systems of the philosophers. I am not entirely pleased to find so many of my favourite doctrines in Rousseau; I should be glad to trace them to a more veracious and less fantastic man. Rousseau had not the respect for concrete fact which scientific method requires. He writes a fictitious narrative, with fictitious experiments and fictitious results. We have even the imaginary deceptions practised by an imaginary tutor upon an imaginary pupil. Can unreality go farther?

But after all it is the good and not the bad in Rousseau which lives and is remembered. A wise man[1] speaks of him as of one "who, without learning, with few virtues, and with no strength of character, has nevertheless stamped himself ineffaceably on history by the force of a vivid imagination, and by the help of a genuine and burning love for his fellow-men, for which much will always have to be forgiven him."

The man whose thoughts run upon improvements in education looks round to see who or what can help him. Some are eager for the

[1] Sir Henry Maine, in "Ancient Law."

support of Parliament, or the County Council, or the School Board; their hope is in official machinery. Others believe that education will advance chiefly by means of Psychology, Pedagogy, and the like; their hope is in academical systems. There are also a few, of whom I confess myself to be one, who trust rather to the spread of the wise and humane methods of teachers like Pestalozzi and Froebel. Education, like other forms of human enterprise, needs new life from time to time, and life can only be breathed into it by the living soul.

INDEX.

	PAGE
Anatomy, Baer's Teaching of,	195
Arithmetic,	57, 69
Arithmetical Precision,	98
Ascham, Roger,	136
Bacon,	153, 156
Baer, K. E. von,	171
Bain on Classical Learning,	138
— on Education,	225
Boys,	54, 76, 221
Breadth,	5
Cabinet,	31
Cambridge and Oxford Local Examinations,	145
Candidates and Examiners,	145
Cardboard Models of Crystals,	31
Chart, Historical,	14
Cheke, Sir John,	136
Classical Grammar and Literature,	123
Concrete Illustrations,	9
Costumes,	32
Curiosity,	210, 225
Darwin,	10, 223
Day, Thomas,	201
Decorations,	31
Deduction,	115
Deductive Geometry,	119
De Morgan's Class,	4
De Morgan on Euclid,	120
Döllinger,	191
Doll's House,	31
Drawing,	92
Edgeworth, Miss,	201
— R. L.,	197, 201
Edgeworths on Practical Education,	197
English Grammar,	60
— History,	10, 57
Epictetus quoted,	243
Eskimaux in London,	202
Euclid,	110

INDEX.

Examiners and Candidates, . . . 145
Examination Questions, 149
Experimental Geometry, . . . 118
Experiments, . . 32

Finding out and being told, . . . 33
Findlay, J. J., quoted, 153
Fitch quoted, . . 159
Frederick the Great, . 173
French, . 56, 58, 130
Froebel, . . . 234

Geography, . . . 96
Geometry, . . 58, 110
—, Deductive, . . 119
—, Experimental, 117, 118
— of Euclid, . . 110

Heine on Latin, . . 129
Helplessness and Handiness, . . . 22
Henry's First Latin Book, . . . 135
Herford quoted, . . 244
Herford's Student's Froebel, . . . 235
Herschel's Natural Philosophy, . . 169
Historical Chart, . 14
History, English, . 10
Home Lessons, . 27, 50, 64
Homer, . . . 131

Horace, . . . 132
Huxley's Teaching, 193

Induction, . . . 115
Interesting, Necessity of being, . . . 2

Juvenal, . . . 132

Langley on Computation, . . . 109
— on Geometrical Text-Books, . . . 118
Languages, . . 60, 61
Latin Exercises, . 60, 50
— Grammar, . . 134
—, Teaching of, . . 126
Learning by doing, . 38
Lecturers, Maxims for, 6
Lecturing and Teaching, . . . 82
Leeuwenhoeck, . . 223
Linnæus, . . . 182
Locke quoted, 168, 237, 239
Love of Literature, . 131
Lupton on Arithmetic, 98

Map-Drawing, . . 96
Marking Examination Papers, . . . 147
Matthews, T. H., on Teaching of Classics, 123
Mayor, J. B., on Teaching of Classics, . 123
Maxims for Lecturers, 6

INDEX.

	PAGE
Menagerie,	29
Montaigne quoted,	161
Moseley, H. N.,	232
Museums, School,	138
Natural History,	216
Naturalist, Training of a Great,	171
Nature-Study,	209
Necessity of being interesting,	2
Object Lessons,	38, 59, 219, 223
Optics,	212, 222
Oxford and Cambridge Local Examinations,	145
Paper-Books,	30
— Folding in Geometry,	117
— Work,	30
Pedagogy and Psychology,	152
Pedantry,	5
Pendulum Curves,	32
Pestalozzi,	234
Philanthropinismus of Basedow,	180
Photography,	31
Plain Speech,	41
Plato's Meno,	114
Play,	27, 55, 241
Poetry, Learning of,	57

	PAGE
Printed Letters,	29
Psychology and Pedagogy,	152
Punctuation,	45
Punishments,	16
Reading Aloud,	57, 90
Réaumur,	223
Rewards and Punishments,	16, 208
Rousseau,	201, 245
Scepticism,	233
Scholarships,	21
School-Hours,	46
— Museums,	138
— Subjects,	53, 76
Science of Teaching,	158
—, Teaching of,	63, 72, 212
Scrap-Book,	30
Smithells quoted,	88
Spencer quoted,	35
Socrates in Plato's Meno,	114
— quoted,	168
Subjects and Scholars,	66
Tidiness in Schools,	33
Todhunter quoted,	231
Toys,	27, 207
Training of Teachers,	153
White of Selborne quoted,	205

www.ingramcontent.com/pod-product-compliance
Lightning Source LLC
Chambersburg PA
CBHW020756230426
43666CB00007B/714